HOW I BEAT THE
MONEY GAME

HOW I BEAT THE
MONEY
GAME

Unleashing Abundant
Wealth and Transforming Legacies

WILLIE L. DAVIS SR.

ARPress
ILLUMINATING IDEAS
EMPOWERING VOICES

ARPress
45 Dan Road Suite 5
Canton MA 02021
Hotline: 1(888) 821-0229
Fax: 1(508) 545-7580

Ordering Information:
Quantity sales. Special discounts are available on quantity purchases by corporations, associations, and others. For details, contact the publisher at the address above.

Printed in the United States of America.

ISBN-13:   Softcover   979-8-89330-715-3
                   eBook   979-8-89330-716-0
Library of Congress Control Number: 2024902678

TABLE OF CONTENTS

To all the overcomers, who refuse to quit and understand that there is no "I" in a team. And to my wife, Aura, our wonderful kids, Teaura, Chantell, Willie Jr., and all my siblings who know what the word "Love" really means.

Thank you.

Acknowledgements

First and foremost, I must give thanks to my Heavenly FATHER, without whom I am nothing. In Jesus 'name. Amen! I've always wanted to write a book because I believe that GOD had given me something important to say. Matthew C. Horne and Lightning Fast Book Publishing have made this a reality. There are so many special people that have helped me along this journey, that I feel challenged to mention all of them without missing someone. Please forgive me in advance if that is the case.

My extended family is so large that I will have to say thank you to the entire Newell Family, for being there for me, keeping a family tradition alive and meeting faithfully every year for the last 56 years. "The Family That Prays Together, Stays Together." Thank you to all the elders of Davis' and Newells' that went home to Glory before us. I also want to thank the Hueytown Class of '73. I want to thank my immediate family, my wife, Aura, my firstborn son, Emealio, my two daughters, Teaura and Chantell, my youngest son, Willie Davis Jr, my brothers, Jesse and David, and their wives, Jessie Lee and Ruth, my sisters and their spouse's: Bettie Davis, Barbara and John Dobbins, Claudia and John Cook (John you are missed), Marilyn & Charlie Felder, and to all my nieces and nephews. I also want to thank Mrs. Virginia Clark, my mother-inlaw, Johnny & Delores Mararac, my other mother and father-in-law, the Manang's Fran, Ela, Tess, Edna, Ida, Lita, Veron, Merivic & their spouses, Linda & Mark Bowling and their family, Tatay Pineda, Drs. Joel and Florence Garcia and Ate Jean and Family.

I would like to give a big thanks to my old and new friends who mentored and helped me along the way: Connie Chao who held me by the hand in real estate; Napa Pomjak my kindred spirit who pulled me out of the fire; Ronald Scarboro, Ronald Cain, Ed Esters, Amos Penny, and Hugh Orgias; my other brothers. Michael Wiedder, Chuck Williams, Pete Hamby, Simon & Frazer Brookes, and my newest but no less special mentors and friends.

I would also like to thank my Sherlock Team including Dr. Lloyd Charles, Kyle Freeman, Miriam Baking, Art and Joy Wilson, Tita Cook, Jeanette Espendia, Gray Shanks, Princess Leah, Carl Johnson, Psalm 1 Victory Foundation, Thunder Williams, Scott Williams,Lisa Timbol, Denver Sanchez, Anh Ha, James Behn, Gigi Balmaceda, Gillermina Knobel, Ofelia Duya, Mark Duya, John Duya, Ligaya Foster, Juana & Bill Taylor, Faith Chiwawana, Remy Ybay, Joanne Williams, TaRessa Stovall, Talking Feather, Sandrine Tengang, Ela Pena, Al Hawkins, Al Mitchell, Nate Davis, Nagaria Davis, Sylvia Reese, Nancy Orgias, Prakit Wesler, Sonya Nelson, Clintonia Paterson, Nelda McHenry, Andrea Montgomery, Kuya George, Pastor

Julmar, and Tats, Ela & Jojit. Inspirers: Karin Parsons, Sherry Tabb, Dino Crawley, Brandon Ivey, Ken Stoll, Mike Mucci, Ron Head, Ed & Gloria Witherspoon, Paul & Alice Gutierrez, Ate & Kuya Velez and Family, Rico & Bing Reyes, Jojo & My My Naguit, Kuya James & Ates Isles & Vivian; Mars & Pars: Elvie & Gary Lancaster, Marie & Danny, Agnes & Glenn Espelita, and Mars Precy & Family. A special thanks to Keith Cayenne who is a brother closer to my heart and more special to me than he knows. I also want to thank Harlin and Diane McWillie; Tanya and Fabian Morrison, Dyrell & Andaiye, and the Maddison family. MS Divina, Dianne Nicole, and Mr. Ronaldo Galleguez; Allan & Pauline Xhyra Palisoc. I am thankful to Bennie and Valerie Fitzgerald, Ed Randle, Sundra Escott-Russell, and the Primerica team. Bennie has been a father, brother, mentor, and friend to me. Thank you to Sir Stevie; Ver & Best; Ann; and Penn (Salad Master Team). Last but not least I would like to thank Mr. Art Williams – Founder of A.L. Williams and Associates – Author of the Book Common Sense.

I wish to thank in memorial: Mrs. Selina Thomas – Grandmother; Mrs. Ella M. Strother – My Mother, "You are always with me!" Mr. Jesse C. Davis My Father –

Uncles: Bill; Pettie C.; Terrance; George; Aunts: Laura, Augusta, Mattie; Florence; Ambrous Lee; and Lela – Helen Grice; Mommy Atayde and Kuya Nonong. Cuz Tom; Baby Sister; Flo; Sterling; Red Tom; Israel; Red Man; Pete; Irazola; Gwen; Caroline; Jean; William; Billy; Don; Mama Julie; Mel and Purvey; Friends: Phyllis Williams and Mr. Ed.

You are missed!

FOREWORD

As a top leader in the financial services industry for nearly 30 years and a Chief Master Sgt., retired, United States Air Force, I've worked with thousands of clients, needing financial assistance and hundreds of leaders. I've spent my entire career helping one family at a time to accomplish their goals and dreams and serving to protect our great country. During that time, I can say with confidence that I've had the privilege to know and to work with, one of the greatest champions of financial freedom, in our times, Mr. Willie L. Davis Sr.

I know Willie because we've worked together for over twenty years. Willie is a very unique individual who spent his entire life, vowing that what happened to him and his siblings would not happen to another family if he could do anything to prevent it. He worked like a man on a very important mission; and was consistently, the number one producer in our base shop. Willie would start early in the morning and stay up late at night to assist his clients with their financial needs.

What Willie recommends is a common sense approach to solving your financial concerns. He never wants you to be average and ordinary. He will encourage, inspire and lead you along the road to financial freedom. He is the Harriet Tubman of the financial services world. He truly believes in the philosophy "Buy Term and Invest the Difference." You can say that he practiced what he preached by retiring financially free of the system at age 49. No, he didn't just quit one job to get another one. Because he believes in multiple streams of income, when he left the workforce in 2004, he was able to say, "I don't have to go to work tomorrow if I don't want to." He could say this with total confidence knowing that he had enough residual income to last the rest of his life, and still leave a legacy to his descendants. That was ten years ago and he is still living his dream life. He has two kids who are doing great in college. The youngest is only 18 years old in her senior year, majoring in Criminology. She plans to have her master's degree by age 21. His kids will never have to work a job.

I know this is what you want for yourself and your family.

Now, Willie tells about how it happened for him and his family!

Wanting to give back to the community, and to give thanks to the Creator for his blessings, Willie started a non-profit, 501 (C) 3, Kid's Charity/Feeding Ministry in the Philippines Islands. He annually feeds over 500 homeless/indigent kids, through his ministry, (https://psalm1vf.org). Willie has unquestionable expertise in finance which he is driven to share. He conducts free money management seminars around the world, at schools, colleges, and universities. He's never satisfied when pain and suffering are going on in the world. Willie has a philanthropic view of the world, and he gives and gives, and gives.

If you want to accomplish your goals and dreams and if you desire to have a road map to financial freedom, invest wisely, send your kids to college, take exotic vacations, live in top neighborhoods, purchase real estate, enjoy a healthy lifestyle, and still retire financially free, then don't procrastinate! Accomplish a financial needs analysis, today! Purchase this book for your library, absorb its contents, refer to it often, and then pass it on to your kids. Get a copy for your friends, loved ones, or family members.

It's one of the most inspiring gifts you could ever give.

-Bennie Webster Fitzgerald, National Sales Director (NSD), Fitzgerald Region.

Introduction

GET YOUR FINANCIAL HOUSE IN ORDER!

If your financial foundation is shaky, then your whole financial structure is weak and unstable. It will eventually crumble and collapse into financial ruin. You cannot escape the fundamental laws that govern money. Believing that the government will always be there to take care of you is an illusion. Establishing your financial plan on sound doctrine will lead you to prosperity. My early environment/ family shaped my worldview and ethical values. They prepared me to win the "game of life." Money once created, like fire, takes on a life of its own. Fire fighters know that once a fire has been kindled, no one knows precisely how it will react to its environment. Money is the same way. Similar to fire it can keep you safe and warm. However, like fire, it can rage out of control, destroying you and everything in its path. If you love money more than the creator of all things, who created the money that you love, then you will ultimately fail. The love of money, and lack of knowledge about how it works, have caused many people to lie, cheat, steal, commit embezzlement, extortion, fraud, suicide, and murder!

Do rich people give because they are rich or are rich people rich because they give?

When I was a child, there was an old saying, "We didn't have a pot to pee in or a window to throw it out of." We were not poor, we were "po". We could not afford the "or" to be poor. We had tin roofs on our homes, still plowed the fields with a mule, and walked everywhere we went. But there was one thing that you could count on. If someone gave you their word, you could take it to the bank. It was better than silver or gold. I mean if Papa Jim told you he would be there at 5 a.m. to plow the field, you could bet your life that he would be there. Papa Jim and his two mules would be standing in front of the house before 5:00 a.m. He already had his first cup of coffee; he was on the job and was working at 5:00 a.m. By the time the sun was getting hot, that field was plowed. Papa Jim and those two mules were on their way back home. It was a time when you could count on your neighbor. Their word and a handshake were better than 10 written contracts.

It was in this world that I was born, and it was out of this world that I emerged with a work ethic, mindset, and philosophical will to win that was stronger than the will of my strongest peers. At my first job, everyone told me to slow down, don't work so fast, you're making us look bad. "Sorry, but I don't know any other way to work was my reply to them." MY MOTTO: Get started early, get the job done, and rest during the heat of the day. Never take a short cut and always do it right the first time. My mother always told me that she wanted me to do great things with my life, but that she loved me no matter what I would eventually become. So she said, "Son I will be proud of you if you become a doctor or a lawyer, but whatever you do in life, always do your best and that is enough. So, if all you become is a ditch digger, then you be the best ditch digger there ever was. You show up on time or before time, never late, start your work when you're supposed to, work until it is finished, and never take a shortcut no matter what or who will tell you to do so. Dig your ditch like there is no tomorrow and it is the most important ditch in the world. Never, ever, let anyone else outwork you. The people in charge will soon recognize you, so there is no need to brag or boast. Stay humble and most of all, fear GOD. One day, the people in charge will say to you, can you show the other workers how to dig like you? This will be your first of many promotions. Next, they will say, since you are so good at teaching others how to dig, we're going to put you in charge of your crew of ditch diggers. After you have learned all that you can, son, you can start your own ditch-digging company!" My mother's advice has proven to be invaluable throughout my life, and it has never failed me. My mother did not have the words for it, Entrepreneurial mindset, but she knew the principle!

In the workplace, I found a different atmosphere and mindset. We would get to work at 7 a.m. or a little later, drink coffee until 7:15 or 7:20, then have a roll call and the morning meeting. At around 7:45, we would go to our duty stations to begin our day. Because I worked for the government, and we had a union, at 9 a.m. we had a 15-minute mandatory break which always lasted for at least 30 minutes. Well before you knew it, it was already 11 a.m. and time for lunch. Lunch lasted from 11 a.m. to 12 p.m., but wouldn't you know it, we had another mandatory 15-minute break at 1:00 p.m. Well, ladies and gentlemen that break lasted another 30 to 45 minutes, and at 3:15 p.m. we shut down operations to do our time cards, because if the paperwork was not done correctly we could not justify all the hard work we were doing all day and our manpower might be cut. Welcome to the world of you're not paying us enough for all this hard work we are doing! I was on the verge of going crazy! What kind of world was this??? There had to be a better way. "They were paying us just enough money so we wouldn't quit, and we were doing just enough work so they would not fire us." Where did this mindset come from?

AN AVERAGE AND ORDINARY MINDSET IS BORN

Let the Government take care of you.

The Deep South 1960's

This was a time to survive and not to thrive! The President of the United States had been assassinated, the conflict in Vietnam was heating up, and the southern public schools were still segregated. In general, there was little to be hopeful about. Financial Independence was spelled, "S&H Green Stamp collection." Our parents would go to the store buy a little food for the family, get issued the green stamps, bring them home, and the kids would put them in the books.

S&H Green Stamps (also called Green Shield Stamps) were trading stamps popular in the United States from the 1930s until the late 1980s. They were distributed as part of a rewards program operated by the Sperry & Hutchinson Company. During the 1960s, the rewards catalog printed by the company was the largest publication in the United States and the company issued three times as many stamps as the U.S. Postal Service. Customers would receive stamps at the checkout counter of supermarkets, department stores, and gasoline stations among other retailers, which could be redeemed for products in the catalog.

In 1961, Congress enacted a pilot program designed to help both poor people and farmers – the Food Stamp Program. The program was a revival of an idea that had been tried during the Great Depression. In both the 1930s and early 1960s, farmers were producing more food than the nation could consume or export. At the same time, there was a large group of people who were going to bed hungry. On the one hand, the food stamp program was and is a sincere attempt to alleviate hunger but is designed to help farmers as well. During the Depression, people on "relief" – as welfare programs were called at the time – could buy stamps that could be used to buy food. A family on relief could buy orange stamps on a one-to-one basis and the government would give the family blue stamps on a one-to-two basis – that is, $10 from the family would buy $10 worth of orange stamps and $5 worth of blue stamps. Orange stamps could be used to buy any food and blue stamps could be used to buy surplus food.

President Kennedy was inaugurated in January 1961. He promised an optimistic future even though there was a troubling recession going on and surplus farm products were piling up in government storage bins. Not content to wait for Congress, his first Executive Order in February (among many other things) reinstituted a "pilot" food stamp program based on the Depression-era model.

After President Kennedy's assassination, President Johnson requested Congress make the program permanent which they did in 1964. Congress estimated that the program would serve only four million people, but it grew quickly.

•	By April 1965, half-a-million poor people were getting food stamps.
•	By March 1966, that number reached 1 million.
•	By October 1967, it reached 2 million.
•	By February 1969, it reached 3 million.

•	By February 1970, it reached 4 million.
•	By March 1970 - only one month later - it reached 5 million
•	By February 1971, it reached 10 million.
•	By October 1974, it reached 15 million.

Wow! This is the 21st century and the government is issuing us more food stamps than ever! Are we progressing as a society or headed back in time? Is this an accident or a deliberate plan to control the masses?

According to the Department of Agriculture – Food and Nutrition Service 11.23.2013

Total annual cost of food stamp program	$71,800,000,000
Number of Americans using the food stamp program	46,670,373
Percent of population on food stamp program	14 %

Supplemental Nutrition Assistance Program (SNAP)

SNAP offers nutrition assistance to millions of eligible, low-income individuals and families and provides economic benefits to communities. Is this 2014 or 1963?

If we do not learn from history, we are doomed to repeat it.

WE SHOULD WORK SMART, NOT HARD!

Multiple income streams

If we do not focus our time and energy on the changes taking place in our society, then we will be a victim of those changes.

There is now a "Paradigm Shift" that is taking place in the world economy. Jobs that existed in the brick-and-mortar industries are going away and moving to the Internet. Online sales exceeded traditional sales for the first time in history in 2013, and unemployment is still at record highs. If we are not flexible and change with the times, then we are doomed to become statistics of those changes. During the 1990's there were also some fundamental changes occurring in the American economy. By taking advantage of them, I prospered. Identifying today's economic shifts and taking advantage of them will also allow you to prosper. Closing a blind eye and ignoring them will cause you to end up broke and on the government's welfare rolls.

IMMUTABLE TRUTH

GOD can't lie.

Based on the fact, that GOD's word will never return void, I selected a scriptural passage from the Bible and structured my entire Financial Plan around it. My goal was to prosper and I needed a verse that guaranteed that prosperity. I wanted a verse that if I kept my side of the agreement then my plan had to succeed or the foundations of the Universe would all crumble. I selected the following: Psalm 1

King James Version (KJV)

1   Blessed is the man that walketh not in the counsel of the ungodly, nor standeth in the way of sinners, nor sitteth in the seat of the scornful.

2   But his delight is in the law of the Lord; and in his law doth he meditate day and night.

3   And he shall be like a tree planted by the rivers of water, that bringeth forth his fruit in his season; his leaf also shall not wither; and whatsoever he doeth shall prosper.

The results of this decision have been nothing short of miraculous! The following are a few additional rules of life that have been helpful to me:

The Golden Rule: "Do unto others as you will have them do unto you." "12 Therefore all things whatsoever ye would that men should do to you, do ye even so to them: for this is the law and the prophets." Matthew 7:12

Karma: This means action, work or deed. It also refers to the principle of causality where the intent and actions of an individual influence the future of that individual. Good intent and good deeds contribute to good karma and future happiness, while bad intent and bad deeds contribute to bad karma and future suffering.

The Hood: What goes around comes around. It means that whatever you do in this life to other people, whether good or bad, will return to you, though not necessarily in the same way.

"I wanted more out of life and I know you do too!
So let's go!"

CHAPTER 1

WHAT IS THE MONEY GAME

The "money game" is becoming financially independent versus unemployment/underemployment, food stamps, soup kitchens, or just being average and ordinary. Financial independence to me meant not having to go to work the next day if I did not want to, and still having monthly income. Not just any income but an income that was equal to or greater than the income I was working for. So I asked myself the question, "What is stopping me from accomplishing all of my goals and dreams?" "The answer was cash flow!" Plain and simple, I did not have enough income and the salary on my job was insufficient. I needed more income. I knew that waiting for a raise on my job was not the answer. I thought about changing careers or going back to school to get more education, but both of those options were costing me time and money that I didn't have. Employers kept telling me that I needed more education and more experience if I wanted to earn more money and get a higher position. So I went back to school and got a Master's degree. Then, they told me that I was over qualified for the job. It was a game they were playing and I was one of the pawns. It was a nightmare that I could not wake-up from. Do it this way they would tell me, get this piece of paper and you will be qualified, they would say, but at the end of the day I was still underemployed or unemployed. But by now I had a massive student loan to repay, and my fate was still in the hands of someone else. I realized we're playing a money game whether we knew it or not. The real, real rich want to keep control of the world's population and they're using finances to do it. Did you know that the top 1% of the world's population controls 50% of the world's wealth? Here is a quote from Forbes Magazine, 1/23/2014:

"The 85 Richest People in The World Have As Much Wealth As The 3.5 Billion Poorest."

Oxfam International has released a new report called, "Working for the Few," that contains some startling statistics on what it calls the "growing tide of inequality." The report states:

- Almost half of the world's wealth is now owned by just one percent of the population.

- The wealth of the one percent richest people in the world amounts to $110 trillion. That's 65 times the total wealth of the bottom half of the world's population.

- The bottom half of the world's population owns the same as the richest 85 people in the world.

- Seven out of ten people live in countries where economic inequality has increased in the last 30 years.

- The richest one percent increased their share of income in 24 out of 26 countries for which we have data between 1980 and 2012.

- In the United States, the wealthiest one percent captured 95 percent of postfinancial crisis growth since 2009, while the bottom 90 percent became poorer.

Schools, colleges and universities all teach us how to make money, but not what to do with it once we have it. Most high school graduates cannot balance their check book or reconcile their monthly bank statements. Now that we have estatements, and money management programs like Quicken, and Microsoft Money, the art of managing one's personal finances is lost. We just type everything into the computer hit a button and out pops a report. We don't have a clue about assets and liabilities! Money is a total mystery to us and our children.

If a person doesn't know how to manage $2,000.00, then they won't know how to manage $20,000.00 or $2,000,000.00. Did you know that 70% of all lottery winners are broke in five years or less? Beating the money game is no accident! To win this game you need a plan.

There is an adage that I once heard. "If you want to get better you need to play with people better and more experienced than you are." When I was in the military, I was stationed on the Island of Crete for three years. Every year there was an old man who came to live on the beach. He was retired from the Air Force and came to Crete every year with his daughter. They would put-up their tents and live on the beach for the whole summer. I met him one day in the recreation centre, while playing a game of billiards (eight ball). We began to talk about life in general, and how he was living a stress free life, just traveling around the world. He had no financial problems/obligations, no tax worries, and was living a debt free lifestyle. Wow! What a wonderful life style, I thought to myself. That conversation began to shape the way I would view life forever. **Can you imagine living financially independent and debt free?**

After talking with him for a while and listening to him telling war stories he mentioned that he loved to played chess. Great! I said, I like playing chess also. So he invited me down to the beach the next day to play a game. I often played chess with the local players on the Air Station and I thought I was pretty good. So on the following day, I went to play chess with the old man on the beach! To my surprise, the old man on the beach defeated me. It was only by a pawn, but I still lost. Although the games were close, he continued to defeat me for two summers. I would win against the local players all winter and lose to the old man on the beach all summer. At the beginning of the third summer, I couldn't take it any longer, so I asked the old man on the beach, "what is your secret?" "How do you continue to defeat me?" He asked me a question in return, he said, "Have you ever read a book about chess or had a mentor?" I said no. He was amazed and amused at my answer. He went on to tell me, "You are an amazingly gifted, natural chess player, but you are making some fundamental errors." He said I'm a chess master with a 2300 rating and I'm having a difficult time defeating you; (No – I never even considered that he was a rated player) "You only need to read some books about chess. **Knowledge is your key to victory!"**

So I left the beach that day with new determination. I would commit myself to the pursuit of knowledge about the game of chess. I read everything about the game of chess that I could get my hands on, and did not return to the beach or play with the old man on the beach until the end of that summer. Armed with my new knowledge, I formulated a plan. Although, there are a finite number of opening moves/gambits in chess, the list is still formidable. There are many variations to consider, and you can only control what you want to do. Planning to deal with this was a daunting task for me. So, I decided to focus all of my attention and effort on the King Indian Defense. I studied this defense, and studied, and played against myself, planning for variation after variation. Now I was ready to implement my plan. I was ready for the game. It was on a Saturday in late August when I went back to play chess with the old man on the beach. Let the game began! On that

Saturday in August, I finally played the old man on the beach to a draw! A draw - Wow! You would have thought I had won a million dollars, or beat a Grand Master of Chess. Unbelievable! What an accomplishment this was for me. It was a breakthrough in my way of thinking. The old man on the beach, stood-up shook my hand and told me how proud he was of me. It meant more to me than SILVER or GOLD. After that summer, I never saw him again. The lessons I learned on that beach, during those summer days, were invaluable, in shaping my destiny.

KEYS:

I had set a goal, developed a plan, analyzed my situation, and then I implemented my plan. Once I had decided on my course of action (COA) I did not deviate. I allowed for variation, but did not wavier in my conviction to stay the course.

To Manage Your Financial Future You Must Have a Plan

Without a plan you will be like a rudderless ship tossed on the sea of life with no way to control your destiny. Just like I needed to learn the fundamentals of chess, you must learn the fundamentals of money management if you ever want to achieve **"financial independence"**. These fundamental principles of financial independence are not difficult. They are actually quite simple. But they require commitment and conviction. They are not "get rich quick" schemes, but can produce great wealth in a short period of time if implemented early and used consistently. Once you have set a goal, analyzed your current situation, and developed a game plan, you must not hesitate to start your plan. By analyzing your current situation, you can determine where you are at, which is a requirement for knowing where you are going. If you are in the United States, in the City of St. Louis Missouri and want to travel to New York City, you can head "east" or you can head "west". Both directions will get you to your destination of New York City, but going the wrong way will take you a whole lot longer. Some of us take this approach to financial planning. We travel all the way around the world to reach our destination. We will reach our goals if we make a plan, choose our direction wisely, apply ourselves, and don't quit.

My journey to "Beating the Money Game" started with reading a book. The title of this book was, "Common Sense" A Simple Plan for Financial Independence, by Art Williams.

This book explained that most people make the same basic mistakes when it comes to financial freedom:

1. Lack of planning
2. Lack of knowledge about the way savings and protection vehicles work.
3. Dependence on "other people" to be responsible for their financial future (friends, family, agents, brokers and bankers)
4. Procrastination – To put off for tomorrow, what should have been done today.

"Common Sense" also outlined 10 basic principles for accomplishing your goals:

1. Get started now.
2. Pay yourself first.
3. Use time and consistency.
4. Establish an emergency fund.
5. Buy the right life insurance.
6. Minimize taxes with an IRA.
7. Become an owner, not a loaner.
8. Invest with professional management.
9. Start a family tradition.
10. Develop a winning attitude.

It is similar to the situation where I was determined to learn all that I could about chess and apply it to my game. You must learn the fundamentals of the **"money game"** and apply them to your life.

Money seems to have a will of its own. Managing money is like caring for a wilful child. You will either take control of money or money will take control of you. The first step in controlling money is to establish a budget. I know that, for most of you, "budgeting" is a dirty word, but it does not have to be. Today, there are budgeting programs, free software you can get on the Internet, or professional planners that can help you. When I started budgeting, we (my wife and I) took several envelopes and labelled them: Mortgage; Electric; Water; Telephone; Cable; Entertainment; Vacations etc.… We then divided the household income each month between these envelopes. If the entertainment envelope ran out by the 20th of the month, then we did not take money from the other envelopes. We just found other ways of entertaining the family without going out to dinner or to a movie. To establish the amounts to set aside for each envelope, we tracked every penny of our spending for one month. We were shocked at how much the little things added up. Movies, trips to the mall, pizza, snacks, household parties etc….. The fact is that we are consumers. But if we could save money on our monthly consumables then we would have more money to budget toward our goals. In the 21st century, one of the best companies that I know of to help everyday people to save both time and money is **LGreen!**

To learn more visit: https://app.lgreen.ai/join/psalm1vf

Example: If you are spending $400.00 to $500.00 per month on consumable goods and services, and you found a computer program like "LGreen" that saves you $200.00 to $300.00 per month on average, just think what that would do for your budget. **The two tools that I used to make my dream of financial freedom a reality were network marketing and budgeting using scriptural principles!** Once I completed a Financial Needs Analysis (FNA), I found that I needed an extra $1,500.00 per month to accomplish my goal of true financial independence. I started working with a network marketing company to supply the additional income needed, and to be in business for myself.

I put every dime that I made into mutual fund investments, real estate, and stocks & bonds. We budgeted so we could live on one income.

Let's stop and talk a little about the scriptural principles that govern money, and how they can and will affect your budget. I will not go into the religious doctrine that surrounds tithing. But, there is a real consequence for not doing it. I tried becoming prosperous without tithing and I tried becoming prosperous while tithing. Without tithing it didn't work for me. My car would always breakdown, the washing machine, or clothes dryer would always fail and one thing after another kept me broke. Then I learned the scriptural principle behind tithing and began doing it. In Malachi 3:11, there is a promise to us for obeying GOD and following HIS Commandments: 11 "And I will rebuke the devourer for your sakes, so that he will not destroy the fruit of your ground, nor shall the vine fail to bear fruit for you in the field." But the inverse of this is also true. Break the commandments of GOD and the devourer has access to your finances (the devourer will keep you broke, busted, and disgusted). Please allow me to share this with you. GOD does not need your money, He already owns 100% of it. The tithe is to show that you are not placing your faith and love in the material things of this world. Believe me that GOD will make the 90% go farther than the 100% ever did. Picture this: You are holding a one dollar bill, wadded-up, with your fingers curled tightly around it, into a fist. Now, try to put a $100.00 bill into that hand without opening it. It cannot be done! The dollar cannot get out of your hand, but nothing else can get into your hand either. If you will open your fist and let the dollar out, then GOD can fill your open hand to running over. Malachi 3:10 "Says the Lord of hosts, if I will not open for you the windows of heaven and pour out for you such blessing that there will not be room enough to receive it." The tithe is not for GOD; the tithe is for you! I will cover the physical principles of gravity and magnetism later in the book, but just like they exist and have w world, scriptural principles exist and have consequences in the spiritual and physical worlds. "It's your attitude about giving that counts more than the amount you give! Find good-ground for your giving! (https://psalm1vf.org – a Kids Charity) Don't let anyone put you into bondage about the tithe, it does not affect your salvation, but it can affect your ability to prosper." Willie Davis Here is some food for thought: Why do wealthy people give to the needy? Do they give to the needy because they are wealthy or are they wealthy because they give to the needy? "Most people say, "I barely have enough money for me and my family, I can't afford to give." They need to ask the question, "Why do I only have barely enough?" "Luke 6:38 - Give, and it shall be given unto you; good measure, pressed down, and shaken together, and running over, shall men give into your bosom. For with the same measure that ye mete withal it shall be measured to you again." Mete and Measure: What does it mean? If you give pennies (mete) then you will receive pennies in return (measure). If you want to have more, then give more, and give in the denomination you want in return. If you want to receive hundreds of thousands, then give in thousands, not pennies. After the tithe, the next thing to do is to get you to the front of the line. Pay yourself before paying anyone else. What I did was to start a payroll deduction into my company's 401k program of 10%. The company was also paying a 50% match on my contributions. So for every dollar I put into the pension program, they paid me a 50 cent match. Before I earned one penny in interest, I already had a 50% gain on my investment. The difference that these contributions had on my retirement fund was huge! These contributions were also pre-tax dollars so it helped to reduce my taxable income at the end of the year. By placing away a set amount each and every month, my retirement fund began to increase dramatically. Before making this adjustment, I had only managed to accumulate $1,279.00 in my retirement account in 4 years. After moving myself to the head of the line, and contributing to the 401k program, my retirement account grew to over $67,819.00 over the next six years. That account alone was well over $200,000.00 when I left the work everyday world behind.

In the "money game" there are always going to be emergencies. If we do not plan ahead for them they will destroy all of our dreams, and we will find ourselves starting all over again, every time an emergency occurs. The wise thing to do is to set aside money for these eventualities, so that when they happen we are ready. So, what we did was to establish a joint account at my local bank, under my name and my mother's name. Since my mother did not have an emergency fund there was money available for her also. We did not rely on this money for anything else. It was there just for emergencies. Note: When we did not have the emergency fund and were not tithing, emergencies seemed to pop up every month: the car was breaking down constantly, the refrigerator would go out, the A/C unit would quit, the kids were getting sick, you name it and it was happening in our lives. After we set this plan into motion and purposed that we would obey the scriptural principles of GOD that govern money, these dream destroying occurrences ceased in our lives.

Two things that I knew for sure! Number one, I would either live to see my goals and dreams come true or Number two, I would die prematurely. If I were to die before seeing my dream of financial independence come true, I still wanted financial freedom for my wife and kids. I already had a $200,000.00 life insurance policy and I purchased an additional $200,000.00 term life insurance policy for around $44.00 per month. I also had mortgages redemption insurance to pay off the mortgages on our real estate holdings. Now, if I died my family would receive $400,000.00 in cash, and would also be debt free, with the home and other mortgage paid off. They could invest the $400,000.00 at around 10% with an annual income of $40,000.00 per year without touching the principle. They would also be receiving income from the rental properties, all of which would be positive cash flow, with no mortgages. At my wife's passing, the next generation would receive the $400,000.00 cash, and the rental properties as part of our estate, creating a family tradition of giving the next generation a head start in the "Money Game." I knew that I did not want to live and to die, average and ordinary and that I wanted to leave a legacy to my family. But, like a bolt of lightning from a clear sky, my world was shaken, one day. I thought I was getting over on the system, when I realized that I was just another victim of the system. A pawn, we might say in the money game. I realized that there were people and forces far above me who were creating and controlling my reality. I was living an illusion and living in a dream state created by the powers to be.

Chapter 2

The Wake Up Call

My wakeup call came when I was 28 years old. I had just separated from the military, was trying to attend college, drawing unemployment, and acting like I was looking for a job. To keep drawing unemployment, I was required to go on at least three job interviews per week. Therefore, I went down to the local unemployment office to search their data base for leads. While I was there, I read a little advertisement that simply said, "Earn while you learn – Securities and Investment Industry," and gave a phone number to call for an interview. Having procrastinated all week, I needed to go on an interview the next day, to complete my three interviews for the week, and they wanted to interview someone. Awesome, I thought to myself, this is a match made in heaven. I will go on the interview, meet my quota, and just keep cruising through the system. I called and made an appointment for the next day. When I arrived at the location, it was not at all what I had expected in my mind's eye. It wasn't a one on one interview but a group presentation. The presenter looked like he had just stepped out of Gentleman's Quarterly (GQ) magazine. He was wearing a Brooks Brothers three piece, pin striped navy-blue suit, monogrammed French cuffs with his initials on them, diamond cuff links, black wing tipped Stacy Adam's shoes, and although he was a young man around 40, his hair was all white, but not one strand of hair was out of place. He was wearing a necktie with a diamond studded pin, a Rolex watch on his left wrist and what looked like a super bowl ring on his right ring finger. I was very impressed to say the least! All I had known for the past ten years were green military uniforms, dirty finger nails, smelly jet fuel, engine oil and hydraulic fluid. This was a whole new world to me! But, a world that I would learn to master.

Bob (full name Robert) gave that presentation and it blew my mind. Wow! What a slap in the face. I was shocked into reality. My dream state was over. There was another world out there and I did not have a clue about it. From the time that I was a child, my parents would say, "Billy (my nick name) go to school and get a good education so that you can get a good JOB" (Journey of the Broke). I joined the military right out of high school and had spent the last few years of my life, mainly as an aircraft mechanic and later on as a computer operator.

What Bob shared on that day changed my life forever. Here is a copy of the form that Bob had us to fill out. Fill it out for yourself right now; don't wait:

Take out a sheet of paper:

1. How long have you been working in years?_____

2. What was your average salary per year? $_____

3. Now multiply line 1 times line 2. Enter here: _____

4. How much money do you have in savings? $ _____

5. Subtract line 4 from line 3. Place total here: $ _____

What happened to all that other money?

These are my results:

I had been working for ten (10) years and had averaged about $10,000.00 per year.

I had earned around $100,000.00, and I had $5,000.00 in the bank. That was a difference of $95,000.00 and I didn't know where the other money had gone. Bob told us if we did not do something different over the next 10 to 30 years, that we would retire broke or die on the JOB, broke. **That was my call to action**! I had left home when I was eighteen years old with no money in my pockets, no house and no car. Now I found myself 10 years later, with no home, no money in my pockets, and an old car that I owed more than what it was worth. I did not have any credit and could not even buy furniture for my apartment. So I had to take the $5,000.00 out of the bank to get a place to stay and buy furniture. At this rate, I would truly die broke with nothing to show for my efforts.

So I filled out an application to work with Bob. I thought, it would be like the military, take the JOB and at the end of the month the company would pay me. The military had made me blind and dependent on it for everything. The military furnished me food, clothing and shelter, plus a salary. At 28 years old, I had never paid rent or a utility bill. But this was not like your regular old JOB; and like I said, this was a different world for me. Bob told me I had to pay to work with his company. What! Pay for a JOB! There was a $250.00, APPLICATION FEE, and I would still have to buy my own study materials, and pay for the insurance/ securities exams I had to take and pass, to become licensed with the State Life Insurance Commissioner, and the U.S. Securities and Exchange Commission (SEC). Bob said this was a concept called Network/Multilevel Marketing (MLM), where you are in business for yourself, but not by yourself. The company sold term life insurance and coupled it with an investment in mutual funds or annuities. The concept was brilliant but many of the agents failed to practice what they preached. GOD blessed me and I was not among that group.

When I showed up to work at Bob's office, he told me that I needed to study to get an insurance license first. I took the exam, passed and got the license one week later, which amazed the older agents in the office. However, at that point I didn't know why. I thought to myself, wasn't that the way it was supposed to happen? I was very naïve to say the least. Now I had the license, but didn't know what to do with it. Bob ask a couple of the older guys in the office to train me but they said they were all too busy. Bob who was the Regional Vice President (RVP), would not dream of training me. He did not go into "those neighborhoods at night." Even though my friends and appointments were all in base housing, where I lived, he still refused to go on appointments with me. I really don't know why Bob put me on his team. Maybe it was just to see me fail or just to say that he did it. Maybe he did it just to comply with the law. I don't really know, but I'm glad that he did.

In that office, there were six old men who had been around the insurance industry forever. Each of them was very knowledgeable about it, in their own right. Each month they would trade back and forth the title of number one salesman of the month. They would not share their secrets with each other, and all of them refused to help me learn the business. I would go to the office everyday but I was not making any money. In the military, all I had to do was show-up when scheduled and perform my assigned task. I would get paid, every two weeks.

The secretary's name was Lilly and I will never forget her. Lilly took a liking to me and would help me to correct my paperwork whenever I had any. We would chat whenever she was not busy and I was in between self-help videos. Lilly became my mentor, trainer, friend, coach, guide, and ally. I would not have survived if it wasn't for her. One day Lilly whispered to me, "you see John sitting over there working by himself", I said, yes; Lilly said, "go over there and volunteer to help John do his work. Tell him that you are not busy and you don't want anything in return, you just want to do something not to be bored. Most importantly, do not ask him to show you how to do it, just do your best and I will correct the errors."

So I did as Lilly had instructed. I went over and said hello to John, and he replied, "What do you want, can't you see I'm very busy?" I replied, "I would like to help you do your work, because I don't want to be bored and you look extremely busy." John reluctantly agreed at first to allow me to help him. But, when he saw I would do the work for free and not ask for anything in return, John warmed up, he would give me tips and hints so that I could do his work faster. We were analyzing life insurance policies that he had picked up from his clients, during his appointments, the night before. Since I didn't have any clients and didn't know how to make appointments, and no one would teach me, I had plenty of free time. Since I was always around the office with nothing to do, each of those six men allowed me to do their work, and would show me their secrets so I could work faster and faster analyzing their policies. They did not let each other know that I was doing their work, but they would complement each other and smile about their increases in productivity. Even Bob was excited because the office sales were increasing month after month. Everyone was coming into the office late and going home early, except for me. They would not share information with each other but they told "stupid" Willie everything. Each and every one of them taught me everything they had learned over the last 20 plus years about analyzing life insurance policies, making appointments, sales in general, and the securities industry. All my friends called me dumb, stupid and a host of other names, saying "why in the world are you letting those old men use you like that? They are not paying you, they're making money, getting recognized, and you're doing all the work." This abuse from my "friends" and family continued for six months. But my mother's words stayed in my head. "Son be the best ditch digger there ever was, and the promotion will come." Hallelujah!

In the seventh month, I was the resident expert in that office for analyzing life insurance policies, and was number one in sales. What! What! How did that happen they all wanted to know! Lilly did not post my sells on the board, until the month had closed out. The whole office was buzzing. How had this happened, the "office boy" was the number one salesperson! At this point, I had the combined knowledge of all those six men (around 120 years of combined experience), but they did not share their secrets with each other. I could analyze life insurance policies in my sleep; and I knew all the hidden areas and the fine print placed in the insurance contracts by the major companies. During those six months, I had analyzed hundreds of insurance policies from every major and minor insurance company in the industry. What it had taken them two decades to obtain, they had imparted to me in just six months. My GOD had moved in a mighty way. No need to brag about what was done in secret, GOD was now rewarding me openly. Was the pain worth it? You tell me!

We cannot have a testimony, without a test. From zero to hero in just six months. I remained the number one sales person in that office until I left a year later. By the way, I also tested and got my securities license during this time. Since no one else in the office wanted to sell securities in the minority communities, all those clients came to me, so I was also number one in Securities' sales. Oh! By the way did I fail to mention that I was the number one money earner in that office? Go figure! **Hard work beats 90% of the competition**.

Let me share with you a story, a story of **WHY** I was successful and **WHY** I will never **QUIT**!

My father died when I was just six years old and left my mother, who he married at age 17, with six kids and no life insurance to speak of. What little he had went to pay for his burial. My father had 12 brothers and sisters and their solution was to breakup our family and split the 6 kids between my father's brothers and sisters. This was about to happen until one of my aunts said she would take my oldest sister to do her house work and my middle sister to look at because her hair was long to her waist, and her skin was fair. My mother threw a fit and said she would keep us all together. Hallelujah! Praise the Lord.

We didn't have very much money but we had a lot of love. We became known as the family you didn't want to mess with, because if you fought one of us you would have to fight us all, and we would not quit. You want to fight with a Davis, bring your lunch and dinner, because when you get tired of knocking us down, now it's our turn. There is no sense in saying that you want to quit and it's over, because the fight is just starting. With our last ounce of strength or until we could not move, we would continue to get back up. When your hands begin to hurt from hitting me, it's my time. When the sun is too hot for you, it's my time. When you try to run away, I'm faster and it's my time. If you knock me out, don't forget tomorrow is coming, and it's my time. They soon understood that there was no way out, so it was better not to enter into the fight. **Never enter into a situation without an exit strategy.** People around us quickly learned, it's just better to leave the Davis' family alone. It's not the size of the dog in the fight, it's the size of the fight in the dog.

My mother had never had a job, so when my father passed she applied to be a nurse's aide at the local hospital, and was hired. She worked the 10:00 p.m. to 6:00 a.m. shift for 15 years. Can you imagine not sleeping naturally at night for 15 years? She would race home to get us off to the school bus, sleep until around 10:00 a.m. get up and head to a part-time job at a local doctors office. She would then run back home to meet our bus at around 3:45 p.m., feed us supper, help with our homework, sleep for a few hours and do it all over again. I got my work ethic from my mom.

I never wanted to see this happen to another family. It motivated me to get up early, stay out late and do the very best job for every family that I met. Here is a secret: **It's called closing with compassion**. I never sold an insurance policy, my clients would always buy. There is a difference. Not only would they buy the policies from me they would keep them, and tell all of their friends and families about the great job that I had done. Because deep inside, they knew I cared more about their family than just making a sale. I always got referrals and had at least ten more people to go and see after every sale. **Most of the time my clients would call and make the appointments for me.**

I sold life insurance like there was no tomorrow. I wanted to tell every family that I met, "Don't allow this to happen to your family! Don't leave your loved ones to struggle just to eat and survive. It doesn't have to be that way! **I later learned that it was called selling with Passion.** But for me it was a for real life and death situation. My heart broke every time I would think about my childhood as I looked into the faces of my clients' children. If I had to stay up late and get up early it didn't matter, I was going to do the very best I could for each of those families.

The fact is we will either live to see the accomplishments of our goals or we will have an accident or die prematurely. If we die early, we should still provide for our families. We do this by buying the proper amount of life insurance.

Here is another test: It's called the D.I.M.E. It's an on the spot Financial Needs Analysis, but it works.

First, we ask the question, how much money will your family need to bury you?

Second, how much would they need to replace your income?

Third, how much would they need to pay off the mortgage?

Last, how much would they need for the kids' college education?

Death $10,000.00
Income $300,000.00
Mortgage $250,000.00
Education $100,000.00 (per child for 4 years of college)
Total Life Insurance Required: $660,000.00 to $1,000,000.00 depending on the number of kids.

What if one of the spouses had a problem with the total amount of insurance? I would just allow the other spouse to close the sale for me. I would look at the spouse with the question, and ask them to tell the other spouse what it was they wanted to take off the policy. If it was the mortgage, the surviving family members could live on the street or in a homeless shelter. If they questioned the income total, the survivors could beg for food or maybe the kids didn't really need to go to college. Finally, I would say, I guess we could save money by trying to get the State to bury you.

Are you and your family woefully underinsured? ***This is why I wrote the largest policies of anyone working in my office***. I wanted to fulfill the needs of my clients. I would also assist them in setting up a budget, freeing up money to afford the proper protection, and getting out of consumer debt!

DID YOU KNOW?

Out of 100 people at retirement: 1 will be rich, 4 will be financially independent, 5 will still be working, 12 will be broke, 29 will be dead, and 49 will be dependent on family and charity. What about you? Where will you be?

CHAPTER 3

DREAMS/GOALS/PLANS

Beating the money game is no accident! To win this game you need a plan. You need to set goals and act on them to turn your dreams into reality. You need to add action to your beliefs to turn your belief into Faith. "Faith without works is dead." It is your goals that can change your life forever. Dreams are spiritual things, writing them down and taking action on them will make them manifest in the physical world. Think about it, the chair you are sitting on, the book you are reading and the eye glasses you are wearing, at one time were only ideas in someone's head. Your dreams are the same. They are just images in your head. If you do not write them down and take action on them you will never achieve those dreams. The construction of every building starts out with a plan and a blue print of the design. The materials needed to complete the project are considered and the costs are calculated. The whole project is built brick by brick, on paper, before the first spade of dirt is turned. The foundation is excavated to the proper depth, squared and trued, before any work begins. Get the foundation wrong and your whole project is doomed to failure. Fail to plan your financial future and you are doomed to fail. **"The higher you want to go up, the deeper you must dig down."**

"And Jesus said unto him, No man, having put his hand to the plough, and looking back, is fit for the kingdom of God." Luke 9:62 King James Version (KJV)

Once you decide on a goal, or determine that you will undertake a mission, be prepared to see it through to the end. "Quitters never win, and Winners never quit!" Do all of your homework upfront. Know your exit point before you start the process. **Due diligence is the key to success** (due diligence is an investigation of a business or person prior to signing a contract. It is the care that a reasonable person exercises to avoid harm to other persons or their property). In the game of chess, there is a Queen which is actually the most powerful single piece on the board. Most players would rather concede the game than to lose this most prized of all the pieces. While learning to play chess, I noticed this tendency in the majority of my opponents. They were willing to give up all sorts of material losses, to their detriment, just to protect their queen. I learned how to capitalize on this weakness in their games. If they decided to develop the queen too early during the game opening, then I would use all kinds of positional pressure to attack their queen, while developing my own pieces, to their optimum board positions. In order not to lose the queen, my opponents would abandon their original strategy for bringing the queen out in the first place. Once my opponents had chosen this course of action, their fates were sealed. If they did anything but stay the course and continue to develop their pieces without withdrawing, this loss of time and position would eventually lead to their demise. In some cases, I would even sacrifice my own queen if it would gain time and lead to victory. I knew that a knight (the horse) in the right position on the board could control nearly as many squares as the queen; even leaping over other pieces in order to strike. The queen as powerful as she is cannot accomplish this feat, only a knight.

I found that the "money game" and the game of chess are a lot alike. Our opponents are the banks and lending institutions (middlemen). They are trying to out-position us on the chessboard of life. They treat us like pawns and assign very little value to us. They are the bishops and the knights in the money game. The real, real-rich who are the kings and queens are far above even the rich bishops and knights. They live in their fine castles caring nothing about the under classes (the lowly serfs) that also includes the rich. The "rich" are under the illusion that one day they will be superrich, but they are deceived. They do the bidding of the super-rich just hoping that one day they will also be super-rich.

By the time they realize that this is not true, it's too late for them; their prime earning years have been wasted with no real increase in status. The rich compete for political office, and are appointed to the courts, they carry-out the cruel directions and agendas of the super-rich while suppressing the masses. When the wealth of the rich and the middle-classes as a group begins to approach the status of the super-rich, the super-rich will swing into action. The super-rich will start wars, create economic crisis and use famine, disease, or natural disasters to widen the economic gap.

In the Bible there is a story about Jesus becoming angry and throwing the "money changers" out of the Holy Temple: 12 And Jesus went into the temple of God, and cast out all them that sold and bought in the temple, and overthrew the tables of the moneychangers, and the seats of them that sold doves, 13 And said unto them, It is written, My house shall be called the house of prayer; but ye have made it a den of thieves. Matthew 21:12- 13King James Version (KJV). The moneychangers did not just give up and cease to exist after this event, they changed their name to Bankers, and the evil continues unto this day.

There is a big misconception that exists when it comes to money. We think that our goals and the goals of the bankers are the same. Let's examine this supposition a little closer. We set a goal of wealth accumulation. We think that our local banker will help and guide us along the way. We set up an appointment with the banker and keep it the next day. We shared with the banker that we did not know anything about wealth accumulation and we're looking for a safe place to put our savings. As you approach the banker, he reaches out his hand to you. Believing this to be a gesture of friendship we reciprocate by also extending our hand. How was the banker viewing this exchange? We were like a prime cut of New York Steak walking on two legs. He only wanted to touch us to see how tender we were.

Our goals and the goals of a banker are diametrically opposed. The banker is thinking, "I want to get your money for as little as I can pay for it." In today's market environment that is around 1% or less. We're thinking, what a nice man or woman, they're looking out for our best interest, they're willing to keep our money nice and safe and pay us interest (rent) while it's locked in their vaults. Nothing could be farther from the truth. Bankers are in the business of earning interest, not paying it out to the public. What they are really doing is borrowing/renting our money, and paying us pennies on the dollar. I stress this fact and cover it in great detail elsewhere in the book. I mention it here again because the rate-of-return we are willing to accept on our hard earned dollars will determine how well we will do in the **money game.**

The bankers and lending institutions are all very versed in these facts. They are experts at separating us from our money. They are fleecing us and making us feel good about it while they are doing it. The brain washing starts with our parents, continues in the schools and universities, and culminates in our homes when we become working adults.

For our plan to work, we need knowledge and information. Attempting to accumulate wealth haphazardly is an imprudent undertaking. The waters around us are filled with more sharks, con artists, scammers, and just outright thieves than we can count. There are hundreds of books, on the book shelves, that have been written on this subject. The authors share with you theory about how they think wealth accumulation works, but they themselves have never accumulated wealth. They present their theories to us as if they were facts. We follow their teachings and end up worse off than we were before seeking out their advice. Have you ever wondered why that is? It's because they are just regurgitating what they've learned in the colleges and universities. They've never faced the trials and tribulations that come with succeeding in the real world.

To illustrate this point I copied the following from the Internet:

What are the benefits of saving money in a bank?

There are many benefits to using a bank or credit union for a savings account. Here are four of those benefits:

- Earn Interest – Money in a savings account earns interest. So just keeping your money in a savings account means you're making money.

- Safety – If you put money into a savings account you don't have to worry about your money being lost or stolen. Be sure to select a bank or credit union that is federally federally insured – this way if the bank or credit union goes out of business, you can still get your money.

- Record-keeping – It's easy to keep track of how much money you have. You will receive statements showing how much money you deposited and withdrew. Plus most banks and credit unions give you free access to your accounts on-line.

- Withdraw money easily – It's easy to get to your money with an ATM card or by making a withdrawal or transfer in person, over the phone, or on-line.

Now let's contrast the above statements being published on the Internet with what I've discussed with you.

1. Interest – money at 1% interest in a bank will take more than 72 years to double. Our next generation might see it happen to the original deposit.

2. Safety – our money is not in those vaults! And it's the bankers who are stealing our money.

3. Record-keeping and free access – Most banks even charge you a fee if your account is idle. See list of fees!

4. Withdraw – They forgot to mention the daily withdrawal limit, and the prior notification for withdrawing large sums. My local bank had 15 pages of fees. Here are a couple of pages as an example:

Account Maintenance and Transaction Fees	
BPI	
Particulars	**Service Charge**
Monthy Service Charge for Falling Below the Required ADB[1]	
- Maxi-One with Passbook	PHP 500.00
- Other Peso Deposit Accounts	PHP 300.00
- Third Currency Passbook Savings Accounts	AUD 8.00
	CAD 7.00
	CHF 7.00
	EUR 4.50
	GBP 3.50
	JPY 600.00
	CNY 35.00
Monthly Dormancy Charge[2]	
- Peso Deposit Accounts	PHP 200.00
- Dollar Deposit Accounts	USD 5.00
- Third Currency Passbook Savings Accounts	AUD 8.00
	CAD 7.00
	CHF 7.00
	EUR 4.50
	GBP 3.50
	JPY 600.00
	CNY 35.00
Fee for Closing within 1 Month from Date of Opening	
- Peso Deposit Accounts	PHP 500.00
- Dollar Deposit Accounts	USD 15.00
- Third Currency Passbook Savings Accounts	USD 15.00 equivalent
Service Charge per Excess Withdrawal	
- Jumpstart Account (4 free withdrawals per month)[3]	PHP 10.00
- Platinum Savings (no longer offered)	PHP 50.00
- Multi-earner (no longer offered)	PHP 25.00

ATM Transactions	
-"Balance inquiry at other Expressnet member banks, Megalink or Bancnet ATMs	
- Withdrawals at other Expressnet member banks,Megalink or Bancnet ATMs	
Foreign Transactions via Cirrus ATMs	
-Withdrawals of USD 175.00 and below	USD 3.50
-Withdrawals above USD 175.00	2% of withdrawn amount
-Balance Inquiries	USD 1.00

OK, so we've got a dream, we've decided on our goal, we've developed our plan and we're armed with the knowledge that the financial institutions are not our friends. We know the truth. What do we do now? This is where the majority of us become stuck. We say to ourselves that the powers to be are too strong, so it does not make any difference, what we do. This is a defeatist attitude and could not be farther from the truth. God said, "Whatever we do shall prosper." This is the point where we either buy into the lie or we put our faith and hope in the truth.

Once I arrived at this point in my education, I realized that wealth accumulation could be reduced to a mathematical formula (discussed later in detail). I recognized that I was playing against a stacked deck. If I was going to win the money game, then I had to outplay my competition (middlemen and the superrich). I had to beat them at their own game. My secret weapon: knowledge, faith, and total belief in (The Word of GOD).

"For we wrestle not against flesh and blood, but against principalities, against powers, against the rulers of the darkness of this world, against spiritual wickedness in high places." Ephesians 6:12King James Version (KJV)

You do not have to be religious for this weapon to work!

I did not have to rely on middlemen whose only goal was to profit off of my ignorance and lackluster attitude towards achieving my own financial goals. As stated before, this is where we must remove the word can't/cannot from our vocabularies and substitute it with the words of GOD. We must race ahead towards our goals, like there is no tomorrow. Do not worry (taking thought over and over), because worry is not of GOD: Matthew 6:25-34

25 Therefore I say unto you, Take no thought for your life, what ye shall eat, or what ye shall drink; nor yet for your body, what ye shall put on. Is not the life more than meat, and the body than raiment?

26 Behold the fowls of the air: for they sow not, neither do they reap, nor gather into barns; yet your heavenly Father feedeth them. Are ye not much better than they?

27 Which of you by taking thought can add one cubit unto his stature?

28 And why take ye thought for raiment? Consider the lilies of the field, how they grow; they toil not, neither do they spin:

29 And yet I say unto you, that even Solomon in all his glory was not arrayed like one of these.

30 Wherefore, if God so clothe the grass of the field, which today is, and tomorrow is cast into the oven, shall he not much more clothe you, O ye of little faith?

31 Therefore take no thought, saying, What shall we eat? or What shall we drink? or Wherewithal shall we be clothed?

32 (For after all these things do the Gentiles seek:) for your heavenly Father knoweth that ye have need of all these things.

33 But seek ye first the kingdom of God, and his righteousness; and all these things shall be added unto you.

34 Take therefore no thought for the morrow: for the morrow shall take thought for the things of itself. Sufficient unto the day is the evil thereof. **King James Version (KJV)**

"Walk in the knowledge and the light of Truth, and the Truth shall set you free."

Our dreams, goals and plans are fruitless if they do not line up with GOD's Master Plan for the Universe.

"STRESS AND WORRY WILL ONLY LEAD TO SICKNESS AND DISEASE"

It's not how much we make that counts, but if we can enjoy it!

CHAPTER 4

WHAT GOOD IS WEALTH WITHOUT HEALTH

One hospital stay can wipe out a lifetime of savings. Even if we have health insurance; there is no guarantee that the insurance company will cover all of our expenses, or provide us the best care. My grandmother passed away when she was 97 years old as best we could tell from the information that she had given us. She was probably closer to 105 according to a U.S. Census report my sister discovered after my grandmother's death. But the best part of this story is that she was not frail or feeble even at 90. When she was 92, I would have conversations with her and she could clearly remember things that happened the day before or 60 years before without hesitating to think or try to recall the information. She was the oral story teller of the generations of our family. It was an amazing thing to behold! She always told us that the last time she went to see a doctor was when she was 56 years old; and that she was not going back to see another one ever again. Her reasoning was that if she went to see a doctor he might tell her she had something wrong with her. So as long as she was feeling fine, she did not need a doctor. If I or any of my siblings were to become ill, my grandmother would just go out into the yard, picks some herbs, make a tea and we would be fine. There are all kinds of drugs on the market to make us feel better. From helping with an upset stomach to making our brains function more effectively. In my home town there was a

"DJ" (Disc Jockey) and each day he would end his show by saying, "Don't lose your head, after all that's where your brains are!" I think sometimes we lose our heads to the health care industry. They give us a diagnosis, we accept it, believe it, and agree with it. The next thing we know, diseases are manifesting in our bodies. Our brains are filled with plaque.

Our ways of thinking have been shaped by the school system, whose educational agendas have been shaped by the super-rich. The truth is we can "think our way" to **wealth and health**, but we must take action to control our thinking and remove the plaque build up from our brains. The health of our brain is one of the most important things we can do for ourselves. Eating and drinking things that effect affect our brains, is a real American problem. We live in a country of abundance, but we seriously neglect our brains. Let's learn a little more about it:

Ginkgo biloba – "Researchers cannot say for certain whether ginkgo biloba can improve cognitive functions, but they have found that the extract can affect the brain in several ways":

Better Blood Circulation through the brain.

Stimulates widening of the blood vessels, which leads to increased blood flow to the brain and lowered blood pressure (perhaps reducing the risk of stroke).

Reduces cholesterol levels in the blood (excessive cholesterol is correlated with an increased risk of Alzheimer's disease).

Inhibits the aggregation of blood platelets and the formation of clots. This may lower the risk of an occlusive stroke (caused by a clot blocking a blood vessel in the brain) but raise the chance of a hemorrhagic stroke (caused by bleeding in the brain).

ANTIOXIDANT

Curbs the creation of free radicals, highly reactive oxygen molecules that may injure neurons and cause age-related changes in the brain.

Alleviates the effects of cerebral ischemia – the loss of blood flow to the brain by inhibiting the production of toxic free radicals after an ischemic episode.

GLUCOSE UTILIZATION

It boosts the absorption of glucose, the body's primary fuel, in the frontal and parietal cortex, areas of the brain important for processing sensory information and for planning complex actions.

Also increases glucose absorption in the nucleus accumbens and the cerebellum, brain regions involved in experiencing pleasure and controlling movement, respectively.

NEUROTRANSMITTER SYSTEMS

Ginkgo appears to help neurons in the forebrain absorb the nutrient choline from the blood. Choline is one of the components of acetylcholine, a brain chemical that transmits signals between certain neurons.

Slows the attrition of neuron receptors that direct the response to serotonin, a neurotransmitter that reduces stress and anxiety.

Enhances the release of gamma-amino butyric acid (GABA), another neurotransmitter that can relieve anxiety. Lowering stress may reduce the level of glucocorticoid hormones in the blood, which in turn may protect the hippocampus, a brain structure critical to normal learning.

There are many natural herbs and plants which can affect our brain functions and help to clear them of plaque. I just shared this one because I am familiar with it. It is not a claim or endorsement of the effectiveness of this or any other product.

Staying healthy is one of the best thing I have done to increase my wealth. Knowledge about finance has gained me wealth, but knowledge about health has allowed me to keep it and to enjoy it. I also worked with another network marketing company called Xango. While I didn't stay there long, they did introduce me to the health benefits of the "Mangosteen" fruit.

Swelling is considered one of the five characteristics of inflammation; along with pain, heat, redness, and loss of function. A body part may swell in response to injury, infection, or disease. Swelling, especially of the ankle, can occur if the body is not circulating fluid well. If our doctor wants to give us a diagnosis of swelling in the body, he should just put it in layman's terms. (He gives it the medical extension; "itis

- a suffix used in pathological terms that denotes inflammation of an organ.") I know many of us have received these diagnoses; so let's see if some of these words are familiar:

Appendicitis - Inflammation of the appendix.

Arthritis - Any inflammation of the joints, particularly gout.

Bronchitis - Inflammation, acute or chronic, of the bronchial tubes or any part of them.

Bursitis - Inflammation of a bursa pads near the joints.

Cellulitis - An inflammation of the cellular or areolar tissue, esp. of that lying immediately beneath the skin.

Dermatitis - Inflammation of the skin.

Encephalitis - Inflammation of the brain.

Gingivitis - Inflammation of the gums.

Hepatitis - Inflammation of the liver.

Laryngitis - Inflammation of the larynx.

Meningitis - Inflammation of the membranes of the brain or spinal cord.

Pancreatitis- Inflammation of the pancreas.

Retinitis - Inflammation of the retina.

Rhinitis - Inflammation of the nose; esp., inflammation of the mucous membrane of the nostrils. Sinusitis - Inflammation of a sinus of the skull.

Tendinitis - Inflammation of a tendon.

Thyroiditis - Inflammation of the thyroid gland.

Tonsillitis - Inflammation of the tonsils.

The list goes on and on but these are the most common and familiar diagnoses. Most medicines only treat the symptoms associated with disease; they do not treat the root cause of the disease. Mangosteen with over two hundred years of research data, to back-up its claims, appears to go to the root of most medical conditions, "INFLAMMATION!" There are many "mangosteen fruit" benefits, many of which have been utilized for centuries in folk medicine. Mangosteen has been documented to have the following properties: anti-oxidant, anti-bacterial, anti-fungal, antitumor, anti-histamine, and anti-inflammatory. Here are some of the health conditions that may benefit from mangosteen use: aging-related symptoms, allergies, Alzheimer's disease, arthritis, cancer, carpal tunnel syndrome, depression, diabetes, diarrhea, dysentery, eczema, fatigue, fever, fibromyalgia, gum disease, heart disease, high cholesterol levels, hypertension, inflammation, migraine headaches, myalgia, obesity, pain, peripheral neuropathy, seasonal allergies, seborrhea (dandruff), urinary tract infections, vision disorders (cataracts, glaucoma), viral, bacterial, and fungal infections.

According to the American Medical Association, stress is one of the leading causes of illness/disease in the United States. What is disease (dis=not + ease=effortlessness, no trouble, simplicity)? It means that the body is not at ease. When we worry we put tremendous pressure on our organs and body systems. We get rashes, ulcers, heart palpitations, hair loss, obesity, high blood pressure, nervous disorders/break downs, gout, strokes, heart attacks, stiff necks, blindness, ringing in our ears, etc....; Most importantly, many if not all of these conditions, could be avoided with a proper diet, exercise and relaxation.

The food supply is partly to blame for much of the disease in America. According to CBSNews.Com Staff, 60 Minutes episode:

Up to 70 percent of processed food in the American market contains products of genetic engineering, including soft drinks, catsup, potato chips, cookies, ice cream and corn flakes.

Wait a minute, what's going on here? Did you know that much of our food was being genetically engineered? For what and by whom should be the next question.

What you don't know can hurt you!
That shiny can of cola: Is it the same soda it used to be?

The bright box of pancake mix: What's in it? When a bar of chocolate melts in your mouth, can you taste the GMOs?

Genetically modified organisms, more commonly called GMOs, are in a lot of food. That means that many of the items available in a supermarket today – from soda to mayonnaise – contain an ingredient whose DNA, or genetic structure, has been changed by humans or came from livestock fed genetically modified grain.

Genetically engineered crops, mainly corn, cotton and soybeans, were planted on 169 million acres in 2013 – about half the land in the United States available for crops. To break that down, about 85 percent of the country's corn and 93 percent of soy are genetically engineered for traits including herbicide and/ or pest resistance, according to a USDA report, "Genetically Engineered Crops in the United States," published in February, 2014.

"U.S. consumers eat many products derived from GE crops – including cornmeal, oils and sugars – largely unaware that these products were derived from GE crops," a summary of the report said.

Genetically engineered plants with pest-management properties were first sold for major crops in 1996. More than 15 years later, adoption of these varieties by U.S. farmers is widespread, it said.

The prevalence of corn and soy in our food is the reason that many foods have genetically modified ingredients, according to, Emily Stewart, Poughkeepsie Journal.

We are what we eat! Garbage in - Garbage Out! Our body grows because we feed it food; our mind/knowledge grows because we feed it information; our spirit grows because we feed it the word of GOD. Most of our world views are made up of garbage. If we program a computer with faulty information, then ask for a report, the output that we get will be flawed. If we do not exercise properly, feed our bodies good nutritional food, read books, attend lectures, and study the Holy Scriptures then our world view will be skewed.

Okay so we go out and make a million dollars, win the lottery, or get a million dollar inheritance. What now? Are we ready? Most of us are not!

We find ourselves fat, out of shape and overweight, diseased, sick, and stressed out. With the new found wealth we decide to take a vacation; so we have a plastic zip lock bag with twenty or more prescription drugs sitting on the kitchen counter ready to go on our trip away from home. We have several doctor appointments scheduled for the upcoming weeks so we can't afford to be away too long. We've been feeling tired and run down for the past few months, so we're taking anti-depression medication, another pill to make us sleep, and one more to wake us up. We drink five to ten cups of coffee per day, and we're proud because we've cut back to one and a half packs of cigarettes per day, from a high of three packs per day. Our friends and relatives have found out about the money. Our phone never stops ringing, and the inbox is full and cannot take any more messages. Our email in-box is over the limit and new emails are being returned to the senders, and we are afraid to answer the telephone or the door. There is an Internal Revenue Service (IRS) agent who we're on a first name basis with, and we're scheduled for another audit with him, as soon as we return from our vacation. We fit it in between the doctor appointments.

Part of winning the money game is being able to enjoy the money. Quality of life is everything. The little drama I just described above is sad but all too real in most of our lives. The medical and pharmaceutical industries own our lives. They give us pills for everything without curing anything. The doctors drug us to death, and the surgeons cut out the rest! Have you ever really listened to some of their commercials? They tell us, if we suffer from urinary incontinence/overactive bladder they have a pill that will allow us to go to the rest room one less time in 24 hrs. I will say that again, "one less time in 24 hrs." But here are some of the side effects: The most common side effect of anti-cholinergic is dry mouth. To counteract this effect, we might suck on a piece of candy or chew gum to produce more saliva. Other less common side effects include constipation, heartburn, blurry vision, rapid heartbeat (tachycardia), flushed skin, urinary retention and cognitive side effects, such as impaired memory and confusion or it could cause heart problems, liver problems, blindness, or kidney failure!! Although it's uncommon, there is a risk of water retention that results in a low sodium level in the blood (hyponatremia). This has in rare cases led to seizures, brain swelling and death.

I'm sorry but give me an adult diaper. Establish an exercise program. One thing the military stressed was exercise and having a fitness program. Go for a leisurely walk every day. My grandmother even in her nineties would still walk three miles a day. She maintained a garden, which was really a field (1/2 acres of land). She grew her own fruits and vegetables, and had enough surplus to share with the neighbors. She grew corn, potatoes, okra, tomatoes, cucumbers, turnip and collard greens, lettuce and a variety of peas and beans. We canned these vegetables in the summer and had food all winter. At grandma's house, there were apple trees, pear trees, plums, strawberries, grapes, apricots and nectarines. I want to say it was always a joy to go there, but there was lots of work to do whenever we visited. We didn't need to take-out a membership at the local gym.

Part of the reason why I retired to the Philippines was because of the climate, and the fact I could still buy organically grown food, or grow my own food in my backyard. The markets are filled with fresh herbs and vegetables, while all kind of medicinal plants still grow there in abundance. At 58 years old, I attend Taekwondo class five days a week, with my 11 year old son. Last year I fought in competition and obtained my Taekwondo Red Belt. I relax by my swimming pool, eat healthy snacks, enjoy my family, read and meditate on my Biblical scriptures, daily. I give back to the community, through a Kids Charity, Feeding Ministry, Psalm 1 Victory Foundation, Inc. (https://psalm1vf.org), and I enjoy: HEALTH – WEALTH and PROSPERTY.

Often during my discussions about finance my audiences give me that "deer in the headlights stare." They look at me like, "What in the world are you talking about?"

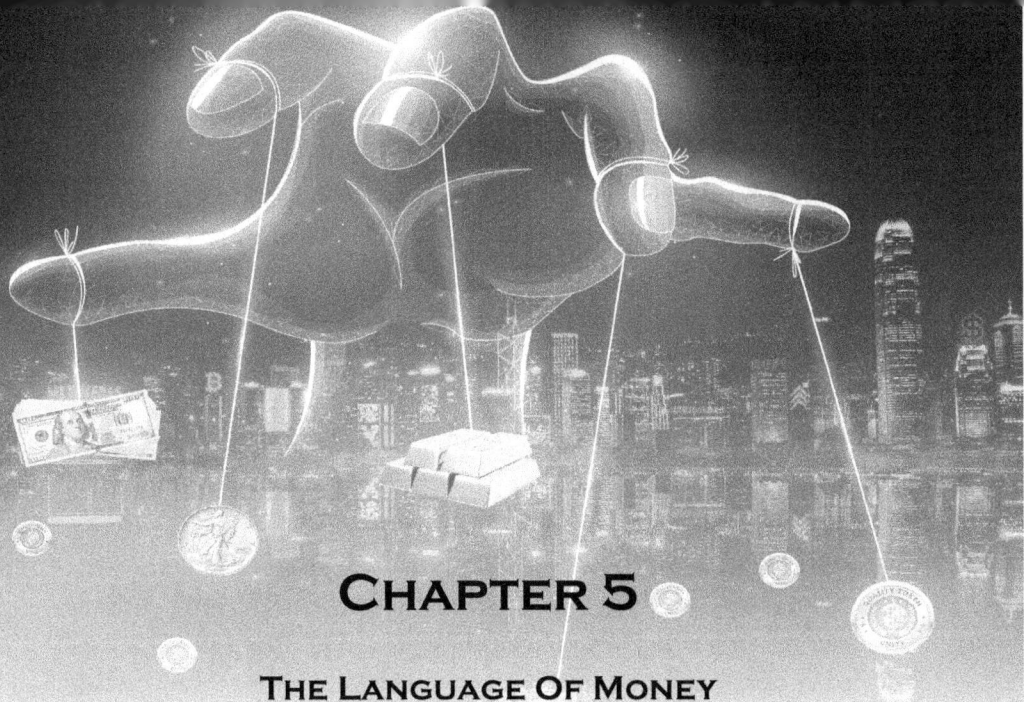

CHAPTER 5

THE LANGUAGE OF MONEY

During our lives, health, wealth, and prosperity are available to everyone. We must come to terms with the fact that the world system operates on money and the fact that the use of that money is a game. I call this game the "money game," and just like in any other game there are rules. The only difference being that in the money game there are two sets of official man-made rules, and scriptural principles regarding its use supplied by GOD. There is one set of rules for the super-rich, and another set of rules for everyone else, which governs the same game. Both set of rules are legal and binding and will affect the outcome of the game. Failure to learn and understand these two sets of rules, and respect the scriptural principles will determine your success or failure in the money game. Super-rich people make the money, write their own rules, control the world's governments, and own the Federal Reserve Bank. Rich people have highly paid advisors looking after their interests, advising them on game strategies, to avoid taxes, the middlemen, and debts. It's like, in a game of chess when two Grand Masters are playing, in the background, off stage, there are team strategists analyzing every move of the opposing player. They looking for any weaknesses in the other player's game, and if any weakness is found it will be exploited. In the "money game" weaknesses are engineered by, your opponent, the super-rich, as a way of separating you from your money! That weakness is lack of knowledge! The solution is: If you cannot beat them, join them. Become knowledgeable and wealthy! Learn their rules and play by them. Remember that both sets of rules are legal, and can be used by either player.

WE DO NOT SPEAK "MONEY"

Think of it this way. Banks and the stock market are like two other planets, and the inhabitants of those planets speak a different language. Going into their offices is like stepping off a spaceship onto one of these planets. The inhabitants of the planets (the banks and the stock market), start to speak but we do not have a clue what they are saying. Not wanting to admit (our ignorance) that we are clueless about what they are saying, we shake our heads in agreement and smile politely at whatever they say: Here is what they just said, "Bring us your hard earned currency and give it to us; we will tell you, "it is safe and secure inside our big shiny vaults." See our vaults here in the background. (But your money is not inside those big shiny vaults. It's loaned back out to other people who take risks with it.) They say to us that they are only financial intermediaries. The conversation continues. Your money will be federally insured while it's in our bank or brokerage account. But this insurance is not what you think it is. Read the small print. We are also going to give you a guaranteed interest rate, but you will be losing purchasing power every year that you receive this guaranteed interest rate. Taxes on your earnings, plus inflation will exceed the interest you earn, so you will have a net loss. Oh by the way, the federal insurance is not dollar per dollar. There is no such thing as "risk free" when it comes to money. The best we can do is to manage the risk. Your money faces several categories of financial risk:

Credit Risk
- Concentration risk

Market risk
- Interest rate risk
- Equity risk
- Commodity risk

Liquidity risk
- Refinancing risk

Operational risk
- Legal risk
- Model risk
- Political risk
- Valuation risk

Reputational risk

Volatility risk

Settlement risk

Profit risk

Systemic risk

(When I was in the military, before deploying to another country, we would receive a "pre-deployment briefing". They told us that if we encountered the local nationals and if we did not understand what they were saying that we were supposed to smile and politely nod our heads in agreement with what they were saying.) The only problem with that scenario was that they could be saying, "I'm going to cut your head off and feed it to the dogs!" This is what happens each time we take our money to the bank or decide to try the stock market. The people at these institutions speak to us in "legal speak". They give us a lot of documents to read and sign, and when we are done signing, they say to us, "glad to do business with you". The problem is, we don't understand "legal speak", but try to fake our way through it, by smiling politely and nodding our heads in agreement with what is being said. We pretend to read the three to five pages of documents, printed in 8 pitch that's so small we can barely see the words. With our eyes blurring, and our heads hurting, we just sign the documents without really reading them. We just want the whole thing to be over with. (Legal speak – language used in contracts to aid companies in overcoming future legal challenges. It provides them with plausible deniability. Plausible deniability is the ability to claim that you didn't do something or say something (even though you did) and have people believe it.)

Where does money come from and who owns and controls it? This is the first question to ask in trying to understand the money game. In the United States of America, we are no longer on the "gold standard" and have not been on this standard, since 1934. A "gold standard" is a monetary system in which the standard economic unit of account is based on a fixed quantity of gold. Some older U.S. citizens still believe that our currency is backed by gold in Fort Knox. Fort Knox is a United States Army post in Kentucky, where the U.S. gold reserves are said to be stored. Our money comes from the Federal Reserve, although despite its name is not owned by the Federal Government!

The Federal Reserve System (also known as the Federal Reserve, and informally as the Fed) is the central banking system of the United States. It was created on December 23, 1913, with the enactment of the Federal Reserve Act, largely in response to a series of financial panics, particularly a severe panic in 1907. Over time, the roles and responsibilities of the Federal Reserve System have expanded, and its structure has evolved. Events such as the Great Depression were major factors leading to changes in the system (The Great Depression was a severe worldwide economic depression in the decade preceding World War II. The timing of the Great Depression varied across nations, but in most countries it started in 1930 and lasted until the late 1930s or middle 1940s. It was the longest, deepest, and most widespread depression of the 20th century.). A Federal Reserve Bank is a regional bank of the Federal Reserve System, the central banking system of the United States. There are twelve in total, one for each of the twelve Federal Reserve Districts that were created by the Federal Reserve Act of 1913. The banks are jointly responsible for implementing the monetary policy set forth by the Federal Open Market Committee, and are divided as follows:

- Federal Reserve Bank of Atlanta
- Federal Reserve Bank of Boston
- Federal Reserve Bank of Chicago
- Federal Reserve Bank of Cleveland
- Federal Reserve Bank of Dallas
- Federal Reserve Bank of Kansas City
- Federal Reserve Bank of Minneapolis
- Federal Reserve Bank of New York
- Federal Reserve Bank of Philadelphia
- Federal Reserve Bank of Richmond

When there's a requirement for additional funds, the Government borrows it from the Federal Reserve and we the people pay the interest. Just like the average public does not understand the money game, neither do the law makers of the U.S., so they are in the same predicament. They receive proposed monetary legislation in the form of a bill but they don't read these bills because they're lengthy and written in "legal speak". So with blurry eyes and headaches, they vote on these bills and pass them into law. Not wanting to show their ignorance about how money works, they're sometimes fooled by the bankers, and witlessly sign these bills into law. At other times, lawmakers are persuaded by powerful lobbyists to pass monetary policy which is not in favor of the public.

To beat the money game we must learn to dance to this music. We don't have to fight against what is happening, but we must learn how to flow with its rhythms. We need to know at all times what is and is not permissible under the law. The laws are not fair, but they are just. What I did was to educate myself about where the rich wanted to go, and either got there first or went there with them. In every state and major city, there is a twenty year plan, also called a Master Plan, but maybe known by other names, depending on the state. Believe me that it will be worth your effort to visit your city, town, or state government offices and review a copy of these documents. Just think of it like a crystal ball. It's a glimpse of the proposed future of where we live (roads, revitalization areas, new construction, subways, airports etc…) I will say it again, know where the rich are going and get there before them or go along with them.

"Give me control over a nation's currency, and I care not who makes its laws."

~Baron M.A. Rothschild

When I started studying for my stockbroker's exam, the first thing I noticed was the language used was not standard everyday English. Even if I recognized the words, the meanings were often different. Have you ever tried to read the Wall Street Journal? Once you finish reading a paragraph, you start scratching your head, wondering, what did I just read? Even in your local newspaper, ever wonder why the business section, is placed between or next to the comics and the sport's pages. If you try to read the business section it will not make sense to you, so you just settle for sports, or Doonesbury! All the information you need to make a decision is there, but it is encoded and hidden in industry language. To win the "money game" become a student of the game, learn the language.

Here is a list of words to get you started:

Vocabulary: Some words or terms, especially those that are common in legal usage, may have different or additional definitions outside of this context.

Asset - is an economic resource. Anything tangible or intangible that is capable of being owned or controlled to produce value and that is held to have positive economic value is considered an asset. Simply stated, assets represent value of ownership that can be converted into cash (although cash itself is also considered an asset).

Bank - is a financial intermediary that accepts deposits and channels those deposits into lending activities, either directly by loaning or indirectly through capital markets. A bank links together customers that have capital deficits and customers with capital surpluses.

Banknote - (often known as a bill, paper money, or simply a note) is a type of negotiable instrument known as a promissory note, made by a bank, payable to the bearer on demand.

Barter - is a system of exchange by which goods or services are directly exchanged for other goods or services without using a medium of exchange, such as money.

Borrower - is an entity that owes a debt to another entity. The entity may be an individual, firm, government, company or other legal person. The counterparty is called a creditor. When the counterpart of this debt arrangement is a bank, the borrower is more often referred to as a debtor. http://en.wikipedia.org/wiki/Borrower

Cash - refers to money in the physical form of currency, such as banknotes and coins.

Check or cheque - is a document that orders a payment of money from a bank account. The person writing the check, the drawer, has a transaction banking account (often called a current, check, checking or checking account) where their money is held. The drawer writes the various details including the monetary amount, date, and a payee on the check, and signs it, ordering their bank, known as the drawee, to pay that person or company the amount of money stated.

Commodity - is a marketable item produced to satisfy wants or needs. Economic commodities comprise goods and services.

Creditor - is a party (e.g. person, organization, company, or government) that has a claim on the services of a second party. It is a person or institution to whom money is owed. The first party, in general, has provided some property or service to the second party under the assumption (usually enforced by contract) that the second party will return an equivalent property and service. The second party is frequently called a debtor or borrower. The first party is the creditor, which is the lender of property, service or money.

Currency - the most specific use of the word refers to money in any form when in actual use or circulation, as a medium of exchange, especially circulating paper money. This use is synonymous with banknotes, or (sometimes) with banknotes plus coins, meaning the physical tokens used for money by a government.

Debt - is an obligation owed by one party (the debtor) to a second party, the creditor. Usually this refers to assets granted by the creditor to the debtor, but the term can also be used metaphorically to cover moral obligations and other interactions not based on economic value.

Debtor - an entity that owes a debt to another entity. The entity may be an individual, a firm, a government, a company or other legal person. The counterparty is called a creditor. When the counterpart of this debt arrangement is a bank, the debtor is more often referred to as a borrower.

Deposit account - a savings account, current account, or other type of bank account, at a banking institution that allows money to be deposited and withdrawn by the account holder. These transactions are recorded on the bank's books, and the resulting balance is recorded as a liability for the bank and represents the amount owed by the bank to the customer. Some banks may charge a fee for this service, while others may pay the customer interest on the funds deposited.

Federal Deposit Insurance Corp. (FDIC) - a United States government corporation operating as an independent agency created by the Banking Act of 1933. As of January 2013, it provides deposit insurance guaranteeing the safety of a depositor's accounts in member banks up to $250,000 for each deposit ownership category in each insured bank.

Fee - the price one pays as remuneration for services.

Fees usually allow for overhead, wages, costs, and mark up.

Financial intermediary - a financial institution that connects surplus and deficit agents. The classic example of a financial intermediary is a bank that consolidates deposits and uses the funds to transform them into loans.

Financial institution - an institution that provides financial services for its clients or members. Probably the greatest important financial service provided by financial institutions is acting as financial intermediaries. Most financial institutions are regulated by the government.

Good - a material that satisfies human wants and provides utility, for example, to a consumer making a purchase. A common distinction is made between 'goods' that are tangible property (also called goods) and services, which are nonphysical. Commodities may be used as a synonym for economic goods but often refer to marketable raw materials and primary products.

Interest - a fee paid by a borrower of assets to the owner as a form of compensation for the use of those assets. It is most commonly the price paid for the use of borrowed money, or money earned by deposited funds.

Markup/Profit - the difference between the purchase and the component costs of delivered goods and/or services and any operating or other expenses.

Medium of Exchange - an intermediary used in trade to avoid the inconveniences of a pure barter system.

Money- any object or verifiable record that is generally accepted as payment for goods and services and repayment of debts in a particular country or socioeconomic context. The main functions of money are distinguished as: a medium of exchange; a unit of account; a store of value; and, occasionally in the past, a standard of deferred payment.

Monetary policy - the process by which the monetary authority of a country controls the supply of money, often targeting a rate of interest for the purpose of promoting economic growth and stability. The official goals usually include relatively stable prices and low unemployment.

Ownership - of property may be private, collective, or common and the property may be of objects, land/real estate, intellectual property, or people. Determining ownership in law involves determining who has certain rights and duties over the property. These rights and duties, sometimes called a 'bundle of rights', can be separated and held by different parties.

Payment - the transfer of an item of value from one party (such as a person or company) to another in exchange for the provision of goods, services or both, or to fulfill a legal obligation.

Profit - the difference between the purchase and the component costs of delivered goods and/or services and any operating or other expenses.

Saving accounts - are accounts maintained by retail financial institutions that pay interest but cannot be used directly as money in the narrow sense of a medium of exchange (for example, by writing a check). These accounts let customers set aside a portion of their liquid assets while earning a monetary return.

Service - an intangible commodity. That is, services are an example of intangible economic goods.

This list is by no means complete and only serves as a quick reference to some of the most often used financial terms. When you hear them in the future you will know where to find them. Learn to speak the language of money. Study it to show yourself approved. Read over legal documents carefully. Have a lawyer review all of your important legal documents before you sign them. Do not rely on verbal agreements. The opposing party will get amnesia on you in a heartbeat. They will say to you later, "if you wanted it in the contract you should have made sure it was there, or else they will say it's in the contract and it's your fault if you did not read it. Trust, integrity, and doing deals on a handshake mean nothing anymore. We live in a litigating society, where you can be sued in the blink of an eye. Do not enter into legal agreements with your friends and family. If you enter into legal agreements with your friends, they will very soon cease to be your friends.

" The rich ruleth over the poor, and the borrower is servant to the lender."
Proverbs 22:7
King James Version (KJV)

CHAPTER 6

DEBT IS THE ENEMY

Hold onto Your Wallet! Debt is the monster in American society today! It's the national nightmare we cannot wakeup from, no matter how hard we try. The U.S. is 33 trillion dollars in debt. That's $73,544.00 for every man, woman and child in the United States. Debt is just another form of slavery, "The rich ruleth over the poor, and the borrower is servant to the lender." Proverbs 22:7

Forty (40) Acres and a Mule

At the end of the U.S. Civil War, some of the slaves were actually given 40 acres of land and a mule to plow the land with. True story! Now the rich land owners did not want to let go of this land easily. So they came up with an idea of how to get the land back. It was called "Sharecropping!" Now those rich land owners knew that the newly freed slaves did not have any money or any way to earn money. So they set up their company stores. The slaves could buy from the store on credit all month long or until the harvest came in. The slaves were then supposed to sell the harvest and pay their debt to the store. But the harvest was never enough to pay the whole debt. So the debt would carry over into the next season and compound at interest. This cycle would continue until the sharecropper died and his children would inherit the debt. When they couldn't pay it off, the property went back to the rich landowner. Do these words sound familiar: terms, cycles, credit, compound interest, periods, debt and installments? The sharecropping system worked so well that the rich land owners did not do away with it.

Today, they call it consumer credit. It works like this: new members of the work force or new college grads do not have much money, so the rich land owners/banks extends credit to them all month long, and they don't need any money. When the harvest comes at the end of the month, (their paycheck) they're supposed to pay off the debt, but their pay check is never enough, so the debt carries over and compounds at interest! This cycle continues until they die. The debt become a part of their estates. When their heirs cannot pay the debt off, the rich landowners/banks take back whatever they owned during their lives.

Everyone wants money and most people do not care how they get it. For these individuals, money has literally become their god. They worship money, coveting the things it can buy, and they are willing to lie, cheat, steal or kill to get it. People are willing to lose their ""Eternal Soul's" for the love of money. "For the love of money is the root of all evil: which while some coveted after, they have erred from the faith, and pierced themselves through with many sorrows." 1 Timothy 6:10King James Version (KJV) No, money is not evil and the scriptures never said it was. By listening to misquoted scriptures, we fall victim to the powers to be. Again it is a language problem. Sometimes we hear words we do not understand, yet do not pursue their meanings. At other times, the meanings have been twisted by the writer, and the meaning is not what we think it is. With intent and study, this language barrier can be overcome. If you purpose to do it you can. People go into all kinds of debt. They mortgage their cars, homes, their kid's futures and their souls. According to the scriptures, a day is coming when we will have to make a decision concerning money. We will either put our faith and our trust in the living God or we will believe the antiChrist and follow him. Don't be deceived by the language that will be used, to woo you into a trap. It will be much like the language used to woo you out of your money. They will promise you the world, yet will deliver you to eternal damnation instead.

"16 And he causeth all, both small and great, rich and poor, free and bond, to receive a mark in their right hand, or in their foreheads:

17 And that no man might buy or sell, save he that had the mark, or the name of the beast, or the number of his name.

18 Here is wisdom. Let him that hath understanding count the number of the beast: for it is the number of a man; and his number is Six hundred threescore and six (666)."

Rev 13:16-18 King James Version (KJV)

What if you woke up in the morning and all your money was worthless? Are you ready? The sign in front of the local store reads we do not accept cash or credit card payments. Present your mark to the cashier when you are ready to checkout. Thank you for your patronage. What would you do? Is your name in the book?

Go to

https://www.youtube.com/watch?v=OjiwSMEqb50

https://www.linkedin.com/thebookoflife

Breaking news:

When is a retirement account not a retirement account?

US Supreme Court Rules - Inherited IRAs Are Not Retirement Funds: in a unanimous opinion written by Justice Sonia Sotomayor, the U.S. Supreme Court on Thursday, 12 June 2014, held that funds from an inherited IRA were not retirement funds that were exempt from the debtor's bankruptcy estate (Clark v. Rameker, No. 13-299 (U.S. 6/12/14), aff'g 714 F.3d 559 (7th Cir. 2013)). The Supreme Court granted certiorari to resolve a split between the Seventh Circuit and the Fifth Circuit (in In re Chilton, 674 F.3d 486 (2012)), and affirmed the Seventh Circuit's decision in Clark. (Certiorari is a Latin word meaning "to be informed of, or to be made certain in regard to". It is also the name given to certain appellate proceedings for re-examination of actions of a trial court, or inferior appeals court. The U.S. Supreme Court still uses the term certiorari in the context of appeals.)

The taxpayers in the case filed for Chapter 7 bankruptcy and sought to exclude approximately $300,000 in an inherited IRA from the bankruptcy estate on the grounds that the money was "retirement funds" under Section 522(b)(3)(C) of the Bankruptcy Code (11 U.S.C. §522(b)(3)(C)).

Bankruptcy Code Section 522(b)(3)(C) excludes retirement funds from a bankruptcy estate to the extent those funds are in a fund or account that is exempt from taxation under Sec. 401, 403, 408, 408A, 414, 457, or 501(a). However, as the Supreme Court explained, although traditional retirement accounts, such as IRAs or Roth IRAs, are included in this definition, inherited IRAs are not because they do not operate as retirement accounts.

Like I said, "When your heirs cannot pay the debt, the rich landowners/banks/creditors, takes back whatever you owned, during your lifetime." Now the Supreme Court is backing them up. And when they start speaking and writing in Latin we're in trouble.

CREDIT CARD DEBT

Master's card! Slave consumer!

What do you think happens to your money when you take it to the bank? Do you truly believe that it locked up in that big vault behind the teller's window, just waiting there safe and sound until you come back to withdraw it? Wrong! It went out in the hands of a speculator who borrowed it from the bank at 5 to 10 times more than they paid you to use it. Yes, that's right you are not saving your money at the bank! The name savings account is a misnomer. Your money is not just sitting there saved in the bank. The bank borrows your money at low interest rates, which are around minus 1% in today's economy. The bankers then loan it back to you or someone else, at 5 to 6% or higher. In the case of credit cards, this can be as high as 20 to 60% APR (annual percentage rate) when penalties and interest are added in. I know that you are finding this shocking, and in some cases unbelievable, but it's true. The APR is always higher than the quoted/stated interest rate. A stated interest of 9% to 15% can end up being 21% to 24% or greater if you miss a payment.

Buy a steak dinner with your credit card and you could be still paying for it 17 years from now. Banks and other lending institutions use a formula to determine your minimum monthly payment.

How a credit card minimum payment works

The minimum payment on your credit card is normally set at the greater of a percentage of your balance, or a cash amount, for instance

3%. Every month interest is added to the balance, as well as the cost of any payment protection insurance policy you've taken with the card.

By the time the minimum payment is calculated, it should cover all of the interest and insurance, and also a tiny part of the money you owe.

The next month the same thing happens again and as this goes on, your debt becomes gradually lower.

But as your debt balance declines, so does the minimum payment, so instead of accelerating the repayment of your borrowing – as you would do in the later stages of a mortgage or loan – you are only repaying a very tiny amount of what you borrowed.

This means that even relatively small balances on a credit card can take an extraordinarily long time to repay.

Here's an example: You have debt of $3,000.00 on a credit card, which charges 16% APR. The minimum payment you can make is 3%. Assuming the interest rate never goes lower, and you only paid the minimum payment, this debt could take over 17 years to repay.

Don't become a slave to your credit card debt

There are ways to make sure that you don't become a slave to your credit card debt…

- Pay as much as you can over and above the minimum payment
  You should be able to do this by a standing order or bank transfer. Anything that you pay each month that's above the minimum will go directly to repaying what you've borrowed, meaning that your debt will be repaid more quickly and cost you less.

- Transfer your debt to a new credit card with a 0% balance transfer offer

Be sure to cut up your old card and close the account – otherwise you risk rebuilding a balance on your card and ending up with twice the problem! There will usually be a fee – somewhere in the region of 3% – for transferring your balance to a new card, but you will quickly repay this since you won't be paying interest.

A 0% balance transfer credit card is especially good if you have trouble paying anything more than the minimum payment each month as every penny you pay goes straight to repaying your debt (and payment protection insurance, should you decide to take it). However, this will only be for an introductory period, so be ready to move on to a new 0% balance transfer card at the end of this time.

FREE CREDIT REPORTS

For decades, the information collected by credit reporting agencies was hidden from consumers. Individuals had no idea why they were denied credit or whether or not their reports contained mistakes. Beginning with the Fair Credit Reporting Act in 1971 and continuing with recent legislation, U.S. citizens have free access to their credit reports and credit scores from each of the three national credit reporting agencies: Experian, TransUnion and Equifax. Citizens also have the right to know exactly why their credit was denied.

Under federal law you are entitled to a free copy of your credit report annually from all three credit reporting agencies - Experian®, Equifax® and TransUnion® - once every 12 months. Every consumer should check their credit reports from each of the 3 bureaus annually. Doing so will make sure your credit is up-to-date and accurate. Each reporting agency collects and records information in different ways and may not have the same information about your credit history.

How to get your free statutory annual credit file disclosure:

1   You may contact the Central Source by visiting www. AnnualCreditReport.com

2   You can request it by phone by calling 877 FACTACT or 877 -322-8228

3   You can complete the Request Form and mail it to: Annual Credit Report

Request Service, P.O. Box 105281, Atlanta, GA 30348-5281

DO YOU KNOW YOUR CREDIT SCORE?

It's not part of your credit report. If you want to know your credit score you must request it separately. Sometimes, there is a small fee.

GOOD vs. BAD CREDIT

Every creditor has its own definition of what is considered "good" vs. "bad" credit. With more lenders today keeping credit standards tight, you need to do everything possible to get your credit in great shape. A low credit score today doesn't have to be permanent. Learn what you can do to enhance the health of your credit.

What Affects Your Credit Score? Wondering when judgments and bankruptcies will no longer appear on your credit reports? Check the dates on records in your credit report. Generally, here's how long judgments and bankruptcies remain on a credit report:

Bankruptcy

Generally, Chapter 7, 11 and 13 bankruptcies appear as public record items on your credit report for up to 10 years after filing. Chapter 13 bankruptcy records are sometimes taken off sooner, 7 years after filing, depending on the credit reporting company's policy. When you receive an Order of Discharge in bankruptcy, your creditors should mark those accounts that were discharged as "Included in Bankruptcy" and they will stay on your report for up to 7 years.

Charge-off accounts

Generally, if a delinquent account is charged-off, the charge-off record appears on your credit report for up to 7 years.

Closed accounts

Generally, negative or derogatory information about delinquent accounts remain on your credit reports for up to 7 years. Positive closed accounts (without late payments or other delinquencies) may appear for longer than 7 years.

Collection accounts

Generally, accounts sent to collections will be listed on your credit report for up to 7 years, beginning 181 days from the most recent delinquent period before the collection activity. A collection account's status should change to "paid collection" once you've paid off the entire amount. If you settle with the collection agency for less, your credit report may list the account as "settled for less than full balance."

Inquiries

When a creditor or lender checks your credit in connection with an application, you'll usually see a "hard inquiry" on your credit report. Generally, these stay on your report for as long as two years, and may lower your credit score slightly. When a creditor reviews the credit report of an existing customer, or when you access your own data online, a "soft inquiry" typically shows up on your credit report. Soft inquiries don't lower your credit score or appear to businesses checking your credit.

Judgments

Generally, most court judgments, including small claims, civil and child support, stay on your credit reports for up to 7 years from the date they were filed.

Late payments

Generally, if you make a payment late, the delinquency could appear on your credit report for up to 7 years.

Tax liens

Under federal law, city, county, state and federal tax liens could stay on your report indefinitely. Generally, after the lien is paid, the record of it stays on your credit reports for up to 7 years from the payment date.

Credit reporting agencies are powerful institutions. One bad entry on your credit report can cripple your borrowing power for years. Even worse, credit reports are often requested by employers, landlords and insurance companies. That's why it's so important to make sure that everything on your credit report is true and accurate. According to a 2004 study, one out of every four credit reports contains serious errors: debts wrongfully listed as delinquent, closed accounts listed as open, debts that belong to other people with the same name, et cetera [source: MSNBC].

I knew that no matter how much money I was able to accumulate, if I was still in debt I would not be free. So, I attacked my debt! I paid off every loan that I had including: consumer loans, revolving loans, student loans, credit card loans, even mortgages. If it was debt I didn't want it!

Beating the money game is more than just getting the highest rate of return with the lowest risk. If you are in debt and paying high interest rates to banks, mortgage companies, and brokerage firms, then you are just spinning your wheels. If your are receiving less than 1% return on your savings and have a 6 to 9% outstanding loan with a credit institution, then year after year you are losing the game. Getting out of debt was one of my highest priorities in beating the "money game."

Debt is the Enemy and Procrastination is its Friend!

You must know where you are at, to find out where you are going.
What's Your F.I.N.

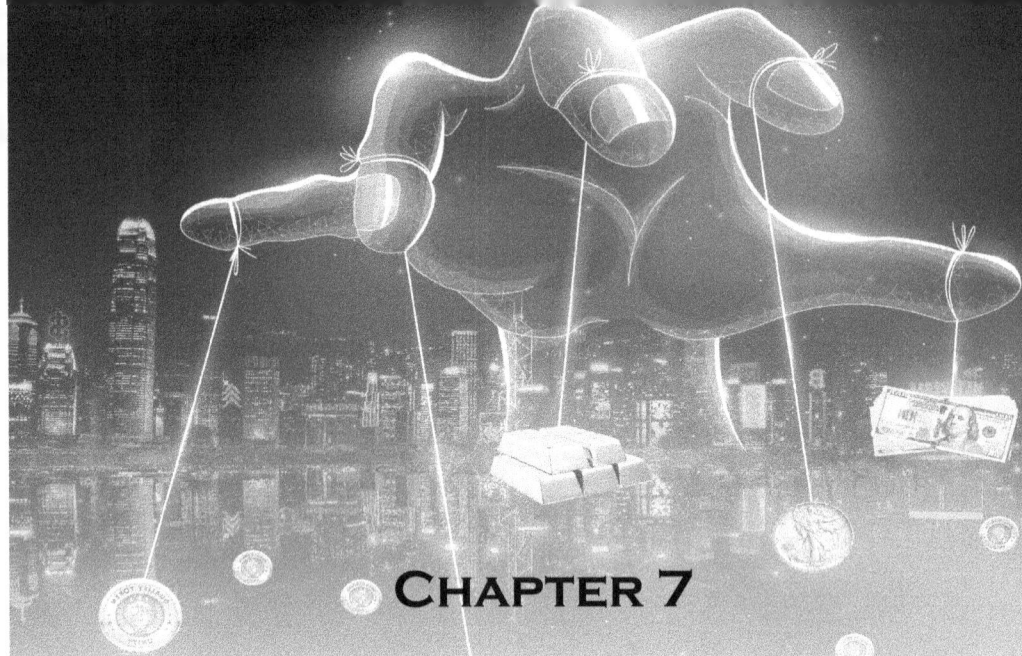

CHAPTER 7

BREAKING THROUGH PSYCHOLOGICAL CHAINS

"FIN"

What is a FIN? Financial Independence Number: FIN stands for the amount of money you personally need to control your own destiny. No one else can supply this number for you. It is a very personal number and only you can determine what it is. Other people can help you with the calculations, but they can only use the information that you give to them. The more detailed and accurate the information that you provide, the better your results will be. It might be 10 million dollars for me and one million dollars for my neighbor.

What is your FIN? You must have a financial plan written down. Writing it down is very important. There are companies and computer software in the marketplace that do a great job of helping you to determine this number. Everyone's FIN will be a little bit different, because one size does not fit all. I owe so much of my success to one company and one man. I cannot help but to recognize him. His name is Art Williams. He founded a company called A.L. Williams, back in the late 70's. That company no longer exists, but its legacy company is Primerica. I worked with this company for over 20 years, and still have many associates in the business of wealth creation and asset management. So much of my success and knowledge came from my association/ relationship with this company, that I must share it with you. I will not try to reinvent the wheel, but I will give it to you just as it was laid out for me. The following excerpts were taken directly from Primerica's website:

Principle #1 – Get Started Now – Procrastination is the enemy.

The High Cost of Waiting

Want to save $1 million by age 67? You'd better get started soon. The longer you wait, the more you'll have to put away each month to reach your retirement goals.

- 27 years old? You have to put away $214 a month to reach $1 million.
- Start at age 37, and you're putting away $541 a month to reach your goal.
- Begin at age 47, and you'd have to put away $1,491 a month.
- Wait until age 57, and you're putting away a hefty $5,168 a month.
- Wait until the last minute (age 62) and you'd have to stash $13,258 a month to reach $1 million by age 67.

This example is hypothetical and does not represent an actual investment. This uses a nominal 9% rate of return, compounded monthly. It uses a constant rate of return, unlike actual investments, which will fluctuate in value. It does not include fees and taxes, which will lower results.

So, the sooner you start saving, the fewer dollars you'll have to put away each month to reach your retirement goals. Don't pay the high cost of waiting!

Principle #2 –Pay Yourself first – Go to the head of the line. If you work on a JOB, start a payroll deduction plan with pre-taxed dollars. You'll earn a fortune in your lifetime, but how much of it will you keep?

Think you don't make enough money to save some of it? Think again!

If you earn $25,000 a year for 40 years, you will have earned $1 million! Earn $35,000 for 40 years, and you've earned $1.4 million.. And if you earn $45,000 for 40 years, you'd have made $1.8 million!

Pay yourself first and you can get ahead in the savings game. Here's what can happen when you save just $100 a month for 40 years:

- At three percent interest, you would have about $93,000.
- At five percent interest, you'd have about $153,240.
- If you got a nine percent interest, you'd have about $472,000.

The hypothetical percentage rates and values are for illustrative purposes only and do not represent any actual investment. Rates of return are consistent nominal rates, unlike actual investments, which will fluctuate in value. Subject to applicable taxes. If fees and taxes were included, results would be lower.

That's the power of paying yourself first! After all, it's not what you earn - it's what you keep!

Principle #3 – Use Time and Consistency – During your years of investing, time will either be your enemy or your friend. Use the power of compound interest as your friend.

The Power of Compound Interest shows how you can really put your money to work and watch it grow.

When you earn interest on savings, that interest then earns interest on itself and this amount is compounded monthly. The higher the interest, the more your money grows!

If you saved $200 each month, after 35 years, your money would have only grown to $148,680 at a three percent interest rate.

At a six percent interest rate, it would have grown to $286,370.

If you received a twelve percent interest rate on your savings, your money would have grown to $1.3 million!

Rates of return are constant nominal rates, compounded monthly. Actual investments will fluctuate in value. Contributions are assumed to be made at the beginning of the month. The chart above is hypothetical and is not intended to represent any particular investment or savings vehicle. It does not take into consideration taxes or other applicable deductions, which will lower returns.

The sooner you start to save, the greater the benefit of compound interest.

Principle #4 – Establish an Emergency Fund – Emergencies are always going to happen in life. It's not if they are going to happen, it's when are they going to happen. One major emergency can derail your entire financial plan. It's a great way to prepare for unforeseen expenses without going into your long term savings. It is definitely your first step in starting your financial plan.

Principle #5 – Buy the Right Life Insurance – Too many people fail to adequately insure their financial futures. The premature death of the primary money earner will devastate the entire family if this very important step is delayed or overlooked. Buy the right amount of insurance while you are young, keep it while your funds are growing and then get rid of it.

"Theory of Decreasing Responsibility"

According to the Theory of Decreasing Responsibility, your need for life insurance peaks along with your family responsibilities.

When you're young, you may have children to support, a new mortgage payment and many other obligations. Yet, you haven't had the time to accumulate much money. This is the time when the death of a breadwinner or caretaker could be devastating and when you need coverage the most.

When you're older, you usually have fewer dependents and fewer financial responsibilities. You've had years to accumulate wealth through savings and investments. At this point, your need for insurance has reduced dramatically, and you have your own funds to see you through your retirement years.

At this point, all you need is a burial policy. Get out of the Life insurance business!

Principle #6 – Minimize Taxes with an Individual Retirement Account (IRA)

There are two types of IRA Accounts: Traditional & Roth IRAs.

A traditional IRA allows you to defer taxes on the account earnings. In addition, you may be able to deduct all or part of the contribution from your taxes if you are eligible. Deductibility depends on whether you or your spouse is active participants in an employer's retirement plan, and on your income. When you begin taking withdrawals at retirement, taxes will be due on the amount you withdraw each year. Withdrawals prior to age 59½ may be subject to a 10% IRS penalty.

Advantage: If you qualify, a traditional IRA allows you to take a tax deduction for the year you contribute – and that means you'll save money on your tax bill. Plus, the money in your IRA grows tax-deferred until retirement. (Note that you cannot deduct your contribution to a traditional IRA if you participate in your 403(b) plan unless you meet income limits.)

Limitation: You will owe taxes on your deductible contributions (the money you put in) and earnings (the interest or investment gains the account makes) when you withdraw the money in retirement.

A Roth IRA offers tax-free growth when you hold it for at least five years and begin taking distributions after age 59½. To be eligible, a single taxpayer's adjusted gross income must be less than $120,000 and a couple filing jointly must have income less than $177,000. The money you contribute to a Roth IRA is aftertax, meaning you've already paid taxes on it.

Advantage: If you are eligible, your money in a Roth IRA grows tax-free, plus you'll pay no tax when you withdraw the money in retirement. If you think your tax bracket may be higher in retirement than it is now, a Roth IRA can help reduce your future tax burden.

Limitation: Because the Roth IRA is only available to people who meet certain income requirements, far fewer people can take advantage of the benefits of a Roth. Beginning in 2010, more people will be able to benefit from a Roth IRA by opening a traditional IRA and then converting it to a Roth IRA because the income limit for conversion will be lifted.

Principle #7 – Become an Owner Not a Loaner – Don't save large amounts of money in your bank account. The truth is you are loaning your money to the bank and they are paying you interest to use that money. The bank in turn loans your money back out at a higher interest rate. Understanding the "Rule of 72" is a must:

The Rule of 72. It's an easy way to calculate just how long it's going to take for your money to double.

Just take the number 72 and divide it by the interest rate you hope to earn. That number gives you the approximate number of years it will take for your investment to double.

As you can see, a one-time contribution of $10,000 doubles six more times at a 12 percent return than at 3 percent.

Years	3%	6%	12%
0	$10,000	$10,000	$10,000
6			$20,000
12		$20,000	$40,000
18			$80,000
24	$20,000	$40,000	$160,000
30			$320,000
36		$80,000	$640,000
42			$1,280,000
48	$40,000	$160,000	$2,560,000

This table serves as a demonstration of how the Rule of 72 concept works from a mathematical standpoint. It is not intended to represent an investment. The chart uses constant rates of return, unlike actual investments which will fluctuate in value. It does not include fees or taxes, which would lower performance. It is unlikely that an investment would grow 10% or greater on a consistent basis, given current market conditions.

How many doubling periods do you have in your life?

Your banker knows this but will not tell you! Just ask them about it!

Principle #8 – Invest with Professional Management – In the early stages of investing, you will not know a lot. So leave it to the pros until you learn. Your local banker is not a professional money manager! So please do not go to them for advice. Today, the internet is filled with advice in this area.

Principle #9 – Start a Family Tradition – Establish a good financial game plan. Write it down. Base it on scriptural principles if you want to be certain that it will work. Encourage your family to save money every month. Talk to your children about investing and set the example for them. In the Bible it says that faith without works is dead. The greatest investment plan in the world without action will not yield any fruits.

Principle #10 – Develop a Winning Attitude – Life will give you whatever you expect, and accept. Ninety-five percent (95%) of winning is between your ears. You must see yourself winning. Don't just want to be financially independent. Live, think, and act everyday like you are already there. Life is a self-fulfilling proposition. Delayed gratification is a word that has been removed from the American vocabulary. Americans want everything to happen yesterday. So they build up tremendous debts trying to satisfy all of their desires. Consequently, they become victims of their own selfish greed. They find themselves with a debt problem with little hope of escaping it. Their goals and dreams seem unobtainable and they become depressed, with a dim outlook on life. But with the right attitude, you can even overcome your debt problems, by using a systematic of approach to eliminating debt. It's called "debt stacking":

By taking into account the interest rate and amount of debt, debt stacking identifies a way for you to pay off your debts. You begin by making consistent payments on all of your debts. The debt that debt stacking suggests that you pay off first is called your target account.

When you pay off the target account, you roll the amount you were paying toward your next target account. As each debt is paid off, you continue this process. Debt stacking allows you to make the same total monthly payment each month toward all of your debt and works best when you do not accrue any new debts.

You continue this process until you have paid off all of your debts. When you finish paying off your debts, you can apply the amount you were paying towards your debt toward creating wealth and financial independence!

I used this process of debt stacking to eliminate and to pay-off all of my debts. It really works! I taught it to all of my clients. I even had some of them freeze their credit cards in a block of ice (that was for the clients who were afraid to just cutup their cards and not use them again). They were also impulse buyers, so by the time the cards would thaw out the impulse to buy had passed. Note: this was before the popular era of the microwave. Smile ☺

CHAPTER 8

LEGACY THINKING

God has blessed me to live in many different countries during my lifetime. There is one thing that I have found to be a constant. The average person wants a decent place to live, food to eat each day, and they want to see their kids do better than they did. Everywhere I've traveled, I have found these same wants, needs and desires. People do not want millions of dollars in the bank, and they do not want to rule the world, all they want is to be happy and to enjoy their families.

To be able to enjoy my family, and to see my kids prosper became my goal/ dream. I wanted to create a LEGACY, I did not want to be filthy rich, but it is possible, and a by-product of winning the money game. I wanted to position myself financially, so if I did not want to go to work the next day, I did not have too. In addition, my family's standard of living would not change. I had seen far too many people living paycheck to paycheck, with too much month at the end of their money, and I did not want to fall victim to that scenario.

They were expending 120% or more of their income on a monthly basis. They were spending every dime they could make then borrowing and using credit cards to supply the rest. They were on a downward spiral with no chance of ever becoming financially independent of the system.

When I was in the military, I lived in what was termed, "on-base housing." We did not pay rent or utilities; everything was provided for us by the military. At that time, I was an E-5 and my spouse was also an E-5, with a combined monthly income of about $2000.00 USD. We were living rent free, but we were still having a difficult time making ends meet at the end of the month. Therefore, the idea of taking a vacation was out of the question. But, I noticed that my neighbor living across the street was going on vacation twice a year. I forgot to mention, I did not have any kids to support, but my neighbor had three small children. Even though he was also an E-5, with a wife who did not work, and three kids, he was still able to go on vacation twice per year. So, in the second year after looking at the pictures that John had taken while on vacation and his home movies, I worked up the nerve to say, "John you and I are the same rank, and your wife does not work, how in GOD's name are you able to go on vacation twice a year, and we cannot afford a long weekend away?" John's answer shocked me so badly, I had to regroup myself! I did not know whether to be offended, angry, mad, upset, or all of the above. Let me clarify, John was a Caucasian, and I am a Black American.

Although we were friends, I was not prepared for what came out of his mouth. John said to me, "I'm sorry Willie but we are not equal." Here is what went through my mind in an instant. What!!!!! You had better get ready to fight. I'm from the south and it's time to throw down. You just insulted me to the bone! Just who do you think you are? Who died and put you in charge of this world! But, before I came out of shock, and before I could open my mouth and put my foot into it; John said, "Allow me to explain." You see Willie, in the "Game of Life" we did not start out at the same spot. Yes, we are both E-5's in the military, but my aunt Gertrude left me a $300,000.00 Trust Fund, so when we started the race (the Game of Life), I was already at the finish line. I'm only in the military because I want to be. I'm just doing my patriotic duty, and my aunt Gertrude made joining the military a requirement for me to inherit the money. ☺

Wow! What a jaw dropping, eye opening education that was (At that time, I didn't even know anyone who had $300,000.00, and definitely had never dreamed that I would ever have $300,000.00 in cash). Snapping out of shock after that bomb shell, I thanked John, and returned across the street, a changed man. That experience with John, changed me forever. From that very moment, I vowed that I would be the one to raise my extended family to a whole new level. I would learn and earn all that I could, passing that knowledge and wealth on to the next generation. They would then be able to say when asked, "How did you achieve this level of success?" "We are not equal," great granddaddy Willie left us an inheritance and the knowledge of how to use it, and what to do with it!

One day while on an appointment to sell life insurance, I encountered the Wang Family. They were a referral from another client, so I didn't know what to expect. When I arrived in their neighborhood it was impressive, but when I turned into their driveway I had to recheck the address that I had written on my notepad. Just when I thought I knew something about the world of finance, the Wang's took me to a whole new level in my way of thinking about finance. This was another mid-course correction for me.

Did you know?

Money turns over in the Caucasian community 2 to 3 times before leaving that community. Money turns over 5 to 6 times in the Jewish community, and an amazing 7 to 8 times before leaving the Asian community. (As an Asian person receives an income, though rarely from a "JOB": They bank with the Asian bankers; use Asian realtors; buy homes in the affluent communities; buy their cars from the Asian automobile dealers; eat at the Asian restaurants; purchase their equipment from Asian vendors; use the Asian laundry services; shop mainly in Asian stores and use another Asian source as often as possible for all goods and services.) Sadly, money often turns over less than one time, in the African American community! We receive our checks and spend the money with the closest vender, more often than not at a 7-11 or another convenience store owned and operated by a person of Asian descent; even though the same product could be obtained at the local supermarket sometimes at half the price. The owners and operators of these stores do not live or spend in the local community. So, the money leaves the African American communities without ever changing hands within those communities. African Americans' are the ultimate consumers.

Although, I did not do any business with the Wang family that day; what they shared with me, I now share with you:

1. First, they told me that they had adequate insurance on all of their family members; and they did, including their 90 year old grandmother who had a 1 million dollar policy. Yes, you heard me right, a 1 million dollar policy! I asked them how they could afford it. They politely explained.

All of the relatives pooled their money together to pay the premium, and upon the passing of the grandmother they would split the proceeds of the policy. They told me that this practice started generations before when their ancestors first came to America. Their ancestors didn't have any money but they wanted to secure a place in the society. So what little money they had was pooled together, and the largest life insurance policy they could afford was purchased on the oldest member of the clan. Upon the death of that member, they would use part of the proceeds to start a business and the rest of the money would be divided among the contributors. This process would be continued, until all family members were in business for themselves.

2. Second, they did not save at the local bank.

3. They had established their own credit union. Any family member with thefamily name of Wang, maiden or married, could join the credit union, but all others were excluded.

4. The credit union provided college scholarships' and grants to their kids.

5. If they needed a loan, they would borrow from the credit union at low interestrates.

6. They patronized their own companies and businesses.

7. They only spent money outside the community when the needed service orcommodity was not available and there was no other choice.

8. They paid all their taxes before they were due.

9. They invested first within the community at all times.

10. They taught these principles to the next generation.

Wow! This family had their own credit union. I was amazed. What! I had never heard of such a thing. To tell the truth, I thought they were having fun at my expense. Later, I did a little research and it was true.

Not only was it true but my family could do it too. (Note: I never did convince my family to do it – we had enough people, we had the money, but not the unity – sad but true). I don't know why the Wang family shared all of that information with me. Destiny, I guess, but whatever the reason I owe them a debt of gratitude. Maybe my humble spirit connected with them on a metaphysical level. Nonetheless, my eyes had been opened to a whole new world, and I say thank you to them. GOD bless.

Here's the biggest difference between credit unions and commercial banks; credit unions work for us, and banks work for their shareholders. Commercial banks that are publicly traded are obligated to act in the best interest of its shareholders. Credit unions are also obligated to act in the best interest of their shareholders, the difference being that the shareholders are the customers. Amazing! Become a member of a credit union for accounts like your emergency funds.

My education about LEGACY thinking continued when I purchased a Housing and Urban Development (HUD) property in a middle class Maryland community, in suburban Washington D.C. After I had moved into the property, I noticed that there was about ten families living in the house across the street. They would come and go daily, all working extremely hard (leaving early in the morning and returning late in the evening). Clients and visitors who dropped by my home would often observe this behavior, and laugh or make rude comments about how they would never live in those conditions. Note: Many of those visitors did not own their own homes, was deep in debt, and lived in apartments. But they laughed at the idea of sharing a home! Go figure! As I continued to observe, various working vehicles started to appear next door.

There were plumbing, construction, vending, electrical, and many other trade vehicles. Soon they put a privacy fence to conceal all of the activity that was going on there. As soon as another house would become available in that neighborhood, those families would pool their resources and purchase that property. Then on a seniority basis, the oldest resident of the original house would move into the new property. This process continued until all of them had their own homes, and my house was now located in a predominantly Latino community. By the way, the scoffers were still living in apartment complexes complaining about the crime and the noise, and how they hated their JOBS!

My Jamaican brothers and sisters had another way of helping each other to prosper. They called it: Susu, which meant collecting and saving money through a savings club or partnership (The name may come from the West African Yoruba or Igbo word esusu or isusu which is translated as a pooling of the funds). This form of saving is practiced throughout the Caribbean and is usually described as throwing hands. Each of the members would pay a specific amount of money, let's say $1000.00 per month for one year with 12 members of the group. If a member needed money for the down payment on a house, it could take months or years to save that down payment. By joining a Susu group, they could have the down payment right away. Each member, when their month came around, would receive $12,000.00 in cash, until the year was up; at which time they would either dissolve the group or start another year long Susu. I have friends who were able to purchase many properties in this manner. The banks would refuse to loan them the down payment, saying that their debt to income ratios were too high. By using Susu, they were able to purchase the houses without qualifying through the banking institutions. You can also turn to this model when facing the same lack of access to capital. Since the market crash of 2008, access to capital has been extremely limited. Even though interest rates have remained low, the bankers are refusing to loan money. For all the advertisement of low interest rate loans, many of us are told on a daily basis that we do not qualify for these loans.

All of these techniques have been passed down from generation to generation. They travel from parent to child, relative to relative across, oceans, continents, and cultural barriers.

FAMILY
IT TAKES A COMMUNITY TO MOLD A CHILD
Family Traditions

A family reunion every year, vacation Bible School every summer, going to church every week, perfect attendance in school every day and communion with GOD every hour.

Wealth starts with an attitude!

For the last 56 years my family, "The Newell Family," has had a "FAMILY REUNION" every year. The tradition started in 1958, after the family had come together to attend a funeral service. My cousin, Ms. Jessie (Davis) Reynolds said, "We only seem to come together when there is a death in the family. Why can't we come together and celebrate life and not death." And so it began. Every year for the last 56 years, on the third Saturday in July the Davis family came together to celebrate life. We would set the location of the next reunion the year before. At first it was at grandmothers' house, in her yard under the trees. We would all bring baskets of food. We would spread the table, eat, drink, play cards, and tell stories all day long. There was so much love and laughter that it would last the entire year until we got together again. We came home from all over the country. Mc Calla, Alabama is where it all started. My relatives would come from Chicago, Illinois; Atlanta, Georgia; Detroit, Michigan; Austin, Texas; Mississippi; Louisiana; Connecticut; California; Ohio; Washington D.C.; Virginia; Maryland; you name a state and if a Newell was there they would come. They came by car, bus, mobile home, train or plane. Everyone knew to set aside the third Saturday in July for the family reunion. My family was so large and was in so many places that we had a family telephone directory. I was in the military and traveling all over the country. The old people would say, "Boy we don't want you going out-there, dating your relatives, and not knowing it." I cannot tell my story about how I beat the money game, without introducing my Family. So much experience, love and dedication went into my up-bringing, that my success cannot be separated from my roots. In my community, any adult could discipline you, and you would gladly take it, praying they did not call your parents, because you would be disciplined again if they did. Meet my family; some of them you may already know:

Legacy

Please meet them as I know them, nicknames and all:

Davis Family – Jesse and Jessie Lee- Kids: Shelia and JeffGrandkids: Bernard, Zack, and Sophia

Davis Family – Bettie – Kids: Paula- Grandkids: Kaylen and Jordan

Dobbins Family- Barbara and John- Kids: Leslie (Brian) Johnathan (Tiffani) Grandkids:

Brooke & Cory Cook Family- Claudia and John –Kids: Lynn (Patrick) & Rodrick - Grandkids: Vincent, Viniqua, Vintrelle and RJ

Davis Family – David and Ruth- Kids: Nathane and NigiriaGrandkids: Dorian Felder Family – Marilyn and Charlie- Kids: Tiesha

Craig Family- Mr. Jerry and MS. Beulah – Kids: Gerald, Andrew, Gloria, Beverly, Janice, Gay, Ruth, Timothy, Louise, Jeralyn, and Jerry Jr.

Crenshaw Family- Gwen and Henry- Kids: John, Henry Jr. (Shirley), Diane (Jimmy), Cynthia, Vanessa, Jeanette, Phyllis (Willie), George (Yvette), Reginald, and Tina.

Mc Willie Family – Mertice, Hardin, Ruby, Faye, Harlin, and Larry

Parker Family- Donald and Augusta – Kids: Flo, Gwen, Don, Laura, Mattie Jean, Carolyn, Augustus, Billy, Buford, and Ralph

Perry Family – Arnittie and Isreal – Kids: Floyd, Ira, Florence (Oscar), Cheryl (Cleve), Mary, and Arthur

Sanders Family – Pete and Irazola- Kids: Laura (Robert), Jackie, Little Howard (Georgia), Brenda (Tony), and Michael (Theresa)

Sanders Family- Tom and Nettie – Kids: Frank, Nat. Tommy Lee, William (Brenda), Jackie, Nicki, and Byron

Sanders Family- Mr. Ned and Ms. Mary – Ned Jr., Clyde, Willie, Mary, Mildred, Charlie, and Joe

Sanders Family- Mr. Vemon and Ms. Edward Lee - Vemon Jr., Mary Louise, Joe Nathan, Cleophis, Evelyn, Doris, Gloria, Larry, and Clara

Washington Family- Momma Julie- Kids Vive (David), Clifford (Bernice) Ike, Bea (Marvin), Dot, and Lou (Ronnie).

Williams Family – Flo and Sterling- Kids: Carol (Lonnie), Michael (Lorene), Jean (Herbert), Ronnie, Ann (Bernard), and Sterling Jr.

Corporate Thinking

We decided that instead of having the reunion in Alabama every year, we would let it travel to other states and bring it back to Alabama for fifth year anniversaries. The national family leadership amended our bylaws to create different Chapters of the Family Reunion in the other states.

Learn to Budget!

When I went to a different state, my mother would just look up the names and numbers and I would call up a relative and go for a home cooked meal, "Southern Style."

Avoid debt at all cost!

What does this have to do with money you might ask? Not so much I would answer, with money, but everything with wealth building! The older people knew how to budget their money. They were frugal with their money and did not spend extravagantly on worthless things. They always had enough money, each summer, to travel home for the family reunion.

There was not a lot of credit extended to the African American community at this time, which was actually a good thing. Our community was not overly burdened by debt. What credit that was extended was at the local store. Years later I found out that the local store was charging 25% interest. Yes, you heard me right! During the 1950's and 1960's, when I was growing up, the bread I was eating and the milk I was drinking was costing my mother 25% interest, every month, not annually, every month. My mother would complain that she could never seem to pay off the bill at the local store. No wonder! The store owner was robbing our community blind. If we did not do business with them, the only alternative was to travel 3 to 5 miles to get to the next closest store. The only problem was that we walked most places that we went. There was no public transportation in Mc Calla. Mr. Jerry Woods, who we called Papa Jerry, had a truck, and would deliver water from the local creek. If we needed a ride to town we could hire Papa Jerry to take us in his truck, which was so old that we did not know if we would make it there and back.

We needed to know how to manage money. Money was so scarce that we needed to budget it wisely. At an early age, we learned the principles of money that our parents and relatives knew. The only thing was their knowledge about "How Money Works," was limited to their surroundings and education. They only knew what their parents and relatives had taught them about money. That's why the local store owners were able to charge 25% interest per month and no one questioned it. Those store owners had the largest house, drove the most expensive cars, and sent their kids to the most expensive universities, in the country; while we struggled just to put food on the table.

PUBLIC SPEAKING!

I learned public speaking in my home church. Every holiday we had to learn a speech, by heart, and recite it before the congregation. These were not just short little speeches, they were three to four pages long. And all the critics were sitting in the audience. Every uncle, aunt, cousin, relative and friend was there just looking at you, waiting for you to make a mistake. It was sort of like the news media today. You can do a thousand good things, but do one thing they do not agree with and you are toast, in the press. We would have to hear about any blunders until the next speech. But it was done in love and only to make us better, never to put us down, or to belittle us. "Boy, you should have seen yourself up there shaking like a tree." The next time I spoke, you better believe I was a rock, strong, well versed and confident in front of my audience.

Vacation bible school was the height of every summer. We would finish the regular school year and immediately start vacation bible school. The bible school was taught by my Aunt Lela. We used the King James Version of the Bible (KJV), and learned all the stories and parables of the Bible. It was my favorite time of the year. Now that I am an adult, I can fully appreciate the lessons that were taught, during that time. Today, I teach a weekly Bible study, here in the Philippines. I reflect on those days in vacation bible school. In the world of finance, I have listened to scores of motivational speakers, mentors, coaches, teachers and many other self-proclaimed financial gurus, but the common theme that they share are scriptural principles. Every precept that they espouse is written in the Holy Texts. I am amazed at the number of people who do not know this, and at the same time I am grateful that I got a chance to attend vacation bible school.

There are Scriptural Principles that govern money! Learn them and prosper – unknowingly violate them and suffer the consequences!

WISDOM

My mother was a stickler about perfect attendance in school, and being on time. Every year we would bring home our perfect attendance certificates and they would be placed into the cedar chest at the foot of my mother's bed, along with our report cards and other school awards. In the Davis home, you did not want to be sick and stay home from school! It would give our parent's permission to practice medicine without a license. ☺ They would go in the woods and come back with leaves, roots and some more stuff, make some teas and potions (poisons), and we would recover in time for school the next day. They would take the fat from a goat (tallow) and make a tallow cloth. A tallow cloth was a face cloth soaked in tallow and heated in the oven. This burning hot cloth would then be applied to your chest, and later pinned inside your tee shirt, so that you could wear it to school. Every fall and at the change of the seasons we would have to take castor oil. If you do not know what it is then you are blessed. As for the rest of us, we all remember this substance that was created in some evil person's mind. If I caught a cold, which was rare, if ever, my grandmother would say, "boy put the castor oil on the stove, I'm going to run that cold out of you. As a kid I thought the virus was so afraid of the castor oil, as I was, that it would flee for its life. I now know that my elders possessed a wisdom that has been lost today. They understood that viruses feed on the mucus in our digestive tracts. So, if they could clear away the mucus and clean out our systems then the virus could not survive, and we would quickly recover. Which we did!

"Nature's secret way to health."

In the Holy Scriptures the leader of the Israelites was Moses. He led the slaves out of Egypt where they had been held captives for over four hundred years. We are captives of the financial system and don't know it. We have been enslaved for many generations. Education is a key weapon that has been used against us. We are suffering under economic slavery, and ignorance of the financial world is the chief culprit. As I said before, all of the knowledge that we need is contained in the Scriptures. This is the main reason for removing the Bible from the public schools and banning the Ten Commandments from public places. There is an all out assault on knowledge and education about Scriptural Principles.

When Moses was old and at the end of his days, his mantle was passed on to Joshua.

1   Now after the death of Moses the servant of the Lord it came to pass, that the Lord spake unto Joshua the son of Nun, Moses' minister, saying,

2   Moses my servant is dead; now therefore arise, go over this Jordan, thou, and all this people, unto the land which I do give to them, even to the children of Israel...

7   Only be thou strong and very courageous, that thou mayest observe to do according to all the law, which Moses my servant commanded thee: turn not from it to the right hand or to the left, that thou mayest prosper withersoever thou goest.

8   This book of the law shall not depart out of thy mouth; but thou shalt meditate therein day and night, that thou mayest observe to do according to all that is written therein: for then thou shalt make thy way prosperous, and then thou shalt have good success.

9   Have not I commanded thee? Be strong and of a good courage; be not afraid, neither be thou dismayed: for the Lord thy God is with thee whithersoever thou goest. Joshua 1: 1-2; 7-9 KJV of the Bible

Every day, I study and meditate on the scriptures. I keep the commandments and guidelines that I find therein. Health, wealth, and prosperity have been my reward for living by these principles.

I challenge you to open your mind, learn from the wisdom of the ages, and know that all the powers of the universe are yours for the asking. "We have not because we ask not!"

COLLEGE EDUCATION IS OVER RATED

Get as much education and learn as much as you can, but don't go into bankruptcy doing it! Let's take a few minutes to look at some of the financial giants in history who did not finish college: Here is a list of the top 100 entrepreneurs that never received a college degree. Many of them you will know while others decided to remain slightly under the radar.

1. Abraham Lincoln, lawyer, U.S. president. Finished one year of formal schooling, self-taught himself trigonometry, and read Blackstone on his own to become a lawyer.

2. Amadeo Peter Giannini, multimillionaire founder of Bank of America. Dropped out of high school.

3. Andrew Carnegie, industrialist and philanthropist, and one of the first megabillionaires in the US. Elementary school dropout.

4. Andrew Jackson, U.S. president, general, attorney, judge, congressman. Homeschooled. Became a practicing attorney by the age of 35 – without a formal education.

5. Andrew Perlman, co-founder of GreatPoint. Dropped out of WashingtonUniversity to start Cignal Global Communications, an Internet communications company, when he was only 19.

6. Anne Beiler, multimillionaire co-founder of Auntie Anne's Pretzels. Dropped out of high school.

7. Ansel Adams, world-famous photographer. Dropped out of high school.

8. Ashley Qualls, founder of Whateverlife.com, left high school at the age of 15 to devote herself to building her website business. She was worth more than a million dollars by age 17.

9. Barbara Lynch, chef, owner of a group of restaurants, worth over $10 million, in Boston. Dropped out of high school.

10. Barry Diller, billionaire, Hollywood mogul, Internet maven, founder of FoxBroadcasting Company, chairman of IAC/InterActive Corp (owner of Ask.com).

11. Ben Kaufman, 21-year-old serial entrepreneur, founder of Kluster. Dropped out of college in his freshman year.

12. Benjamin Franklin, inventor, scientist, author, entrepreneur. Primarily homeschooled.

13.   Billy Joe (Red) McCombs, billionaire, founder of Clear Channel media, realestate investor. Dropped out of law school to sell cars in 1950.

14.   Bob Proctor, motivational speaker, bestselling author, and co-founder of Life Success Publishing. Attended two months of high school.

15.   Bram Cohen, BitTorrent developer. Attended State University of New York at Buffalo for a year.

16.   Carl Lindner, billionaire investor, founder of United Dairy Farmers. Dropped out of high school at the age of 14.

17.   Charles Culpeper, owner and CEO of Coca Cola. Dropped out of high school.

18.   Christopher Columbus, explorer, discoverer of new lands. Primarily home schooled.

19.   Coco Chanel, founder of fashion brand Chanel. A perfume bearing her name, Chanel No. 5 kept her name famous.

20.   Colonel Harlan Sanders, founder of Kentucky Fried Chicken (KFC). Dropped out of elementary school, later earned law degree by correspondence.

21.   Craig McCaw, billionaire founder of McCaw Cellular. Did not complete college.

22.   Dave Thomas, billionaire founder of Wendy's. Dropped out of high school at15.

23.   David Geffen, billionaire founder of Geffen Records and co-founder of Dream Works. Dropped out of college after completing one year.

24.   David Green, billionaire founder of Hobby Lobby. Started the Hobby Lobbychain with only $600. High school graduate.

25.   David Karp, founder of Tumblr. Dropped out of school at 15, then home schooled. Did not attend college.

26.   David Neeleman, founder of Jet Blue Airlines. Dropped out of college after three years.

27. David Ogilvy, advertising executive and copywriter. Was expelled from OxfordUniversity at the age of 20.

28. David Oreck, multimillionaire founder of The Oreck Corporation. Quit collegeto enlist in the Army Air Corps.

29. Debbi Fields, founder of Mrs. Fields Chocolate Chippery. Later renamed, franchised, and sold as Mrs. Field's Cookies.

30. DeWitt Wallace, founder and publisher of Reader's Digest. Dropped out of college after one year. Went back, then dropped out again after the second year.

31. Dov Charney, founder of American Apparel. Started the company in highschool, and never attended college.

32. Dustin Moskovitz, multi-millionaire co-founder of Facebook. Harvard dropout.

33. Frank Lloyd Wright, the most influential architect of the twentieth century. Never attended high school.

34. Frederick "Freddy" Laker, billionaire airline entrepreneur. High school dropout.

35. Frederick Henry Royce, auto designer, multimillionaire co-founder of RollsRoyce. Dropped out of elementary school.

36. George Eastman, multimillionaire inventor, Kodak founder. Dropped out of high school.

37. George Naddaff, founder of U-Food Grill and Boston Chicken. Did not attend college.

38. Gurbaksh Chahal, multimillionaire founder of Blue Lithium and Click Again. Dropped out at 16, when he founded Click Again.

39. H. Wayne Huizenga, founder of WMX garbage-company, helped build Blockbuster video chain. Joined the Army out of high school, and later went to college only to drop out during his first year.

40. Henry Ford, billionaire founder of Ford Motor Company. Did not attend college.

41. Henry J. Kaiser, multimillionaire & founder of Kaiser Aluminum. Dropped out of high school.

42. Hyman Golden, co-founder of Snapple. Dropped out of high school.

43. Ingvar Kamprad, founder of IKEA, one of the richest people in the world, is dyslexic.

44. Isaac Merrit Singer, sewing machine inventor, founder of Singer. Elementary school dropout.

45. Jack Crawford Taylor, founder of Enterprise Rent-a-Car. Dropped out of college to become a WWII fighter pilot in the Navy.

46. Jake Nickell, co-founder and CEO of Threadless.com. Did not graduate from college.

47. James Cameron, Oscar-winning director, screenwriter, and proout of college to becomeucer. Dropped out of college.

48. Jay Van Andel, billionaire co-founder of Amway. Never attended college.

49. Jeffrey Kalmikoff, co-founder and chief creative officer of Threadless.com. Did not graduate from college.

50. Jerry Yang, co-founder of Yahoo! Dropped out of PhD program.

51. Jimmy Dean, multimillionaire founder of Jimmy Dean Foods. Dropped out of high school at 16.

52. John D. Rockefeller Sr., billionaire founder of Standard Oil. Dropped out of high school just two months before graduating, though later took some courses at a local business school.

53. John Mackey, founder of Whole Foods. Enrolled and dropped out college sixtimes.

54. John Paul DeJoria, billionaire co-founder of John Paul Mitchell Systems, founder of Patron Spirits tequila. Joined the Navy after high school.

55. Joyce C. Hall, founder of Hallmark. Started selling greeting cards at the age of 18. Did not attend college.

56. Kemmons Wilson, multimillionaire, founder of Holiday Inn. High school drop out.

57. Kenneth Hendricks, billionaire founder of ABC Supply. High school dropout.

58. Kenny Johnson, founder of Dial-A-Waiter restaurant delivery. College dropout.

59. Kevin Rose, founder of Digg.com. Dropped out of college during his secondyear.

60. Kirk Kerkorian, billionaire investor, owner of Mandalay Bay and Mirage Resorts, and MGM movie studio. Dropped out of eighth-grade.

61. Larry Ellison, billionaire co-founder of Oracle software company. Dropped out of two different colleges.

62. Leandro Rizzuto, billionaire founder of Conair. Dropped out of college. Started Conair with $100 and hot-air hair roller invention.

63. Leslie Wexner, billionaire founder of a Limited Brands. Dropped out of lawschool. Started the Limited with $5,000.

64. Marc Rich, commodities investor, billionaire. Founder of Marc Rich & Co. Did not finish college.

65. Marcus Loew, multimillionaire founder of Loews theaters, co-founder of MGM movie studio. Elementary school dropout.

66. Mark Ecko, founder of Mark Ecko Enterprises. Dropped out of college.

67. Mary Kay Ash, founder of Mary Kay Inc. Did not attend college.

68. Michael Dell, billionaire founder of Dell Computers, which started out of his college dorm room. Dropped out of college.

69. Michael Rubin, founder of Global Sports. Dropped out of college in his firstyear.

70. Micky Jagtiani, billionaire retailer, Landmark International. Dropped out of accounting school.

71. Milton Hershey, founder of Hershey's Milk Chocolate. 4th grade education.

72. Pete Cashmore, founder of Mashable.com at the age of 19.

73. Philip Green, Topshop billionaire retail mogul. Dropped out of high school.

74. Rachael Ray, Food Network cooking show star, food industry entrepreneur,with no formal culinary arts training. Never attended college.

75. Ray Kroc, founder of McDonald's. Dropped out of high school.

76. Richard Branson, billionaire founder of Virgin Records, Virgin Atlantic Airways,Virgin Mobile, and more. Dropped out of high school at 16.

77. Richard DeVos, co-founder of Amway. Served in the Army and did not attend college.

78. Richard Schulze, Best Buy founder. Did not attend college.

79. Rob Kalin, founder of Etsy. Flunked out of high school, enrolled in art school for a time, faked a student ID at MIT so he could take classes. His professors subsequently helped him get into NYU, they were so impressed.

80. Ron Popeil, multimillionaire founder of Ronco, inventor, producer, infomercial star. Did not finish college.

81. Rush Limbaugh, multi-millionaire media mogul, radio talk show host. Droppedout of college.

82. Russell Simmons, co-founder of Def Jam records, founder of Russell SimmonsMusic Group, Phat Farm fashions, bestselling author. Did not finish college.

83. S. Daniel Abraham, founder of Slim-Fast, billionaire. Did not attend college.

84. Sean John Combs, entertainer, producer, fashion designer, and entrepreneur. Never finished college.

85. Shawn Fanning, developer of Napster. Dropped out of college at the age of 19.

86. Simon Cowell, TV producer, music judge, American Idol, The X Factor, and Britain's Got Talent. High school dropout.

87. Steve Madden, shoe designer. Dropped out of college.

88. Steve Wozniak, co-founder of Apple, billionaire. Did not complete college.

89. Ted Murphy, founder of social media company Izea Entertainment. Dropped out of college.

90. Theodore Waitt, billionaire founder of Gateway Computers. Dropped out of college to start Gateway – one semester before graduating.

91. Thomas Edison, inventor of the lightbulb, phonograph, and more. Primarily home-schooled, then joined the railroad when he was only 12.

92. Tom Anderson, co-founder and "friend" of MySpace. Dropped out of high school.

93. Ty Warner, billionaire developer of Beanie Babies, real estate investor, and hotel owner. Dropped out of college.

94. Vidal Sassoon, founder of Vidal Sassoon, multimillionaire. Dropped out of highschool.

95. W. Clement Stone, multimillionaire insurance man, author, founder of Success magazine. Dropped out of elementary school. Later attended high school, graduating. Attended but did not finish college.

96. W.T. Grant, founder of W.T. Grant department stores, multimillionaire. Dropped out of high school.

97. Wally "Famous" Amos, multimillionaire entrepreneur, author, talent agent, founder of Famous Amos cookies. Left high school at 17 to join the Air Force.

98. Walt Disney, founder of the Walt Disney Company. Dropped out of highschool at 16.

99. Wolfgang Puck, chef, owner of 16 restaurants and 80 bistros. Quit school at the age of 14.

100. Y.C. Wang, billionaire founder of Formosa Plastics. Did not attend highschool. Paul Hudson via Young Entrepreneur.

Allow me to share with you a little bit about a Legacy company. A.L. Williams and Associates, mentioned in the previous chapter, was born with 85 people in Atlanta, Ga. and grew to an army of over 225,000 at its peak. It was a company that changed an industry, and it changed my way of thinking. I didn't need twenty college degrees, a business suit from Brookes Brothers, a fancy office, or a Rolls Royce car. All I needed was passion for what I did. Here is a quote from Mr. Williams, "Building big teams requires you having passion about what you do. It's got to be more than just about money." These words ignited a fire in me and they resonated with my spirit. I wanted more out of life and I was going to think my way to it. I would not be average and ordinary. I would sacrifice current wants and desires for future gratification. My kids would have more than I ever dreamed about. Mr. Williams had shown that the improbable was possible; and if he could do it for himself and his family then why couldn't I do it for me and my family?

Although, I have two master degrees, neither of them are in finance. I spent over 20 years working and prospering in the financial services industry without a degree in finance. Luckily, the military paid my complete educational expenses, and I did not end up in debt with a bunch of student loans. If I had just focused on working within my degree fields and earning a living, I would not be publishing this book today. Attending the university taught me how to make money, but not what to do with it once I had it. Universities are great networking opportunities, and centers of learning, but they do not prepare you for the "game of life"!

"A good man leaveth an inheritance to his children's children: and the wealth of the sinner is laid up for the just" (Proverbs 13:22 KJV).

The LEGACY THAT I WOULD LIKE TO LEAVE TO MY CHILDREN IS: "KNOWLEDGE

AND MULTIPLE STREAMS OF INCOME ARE THE KEYS" "SCRIPTUAL PRINCIPLES ARE

THE HIDDEN HANDS WHICH TURN THE KEY"

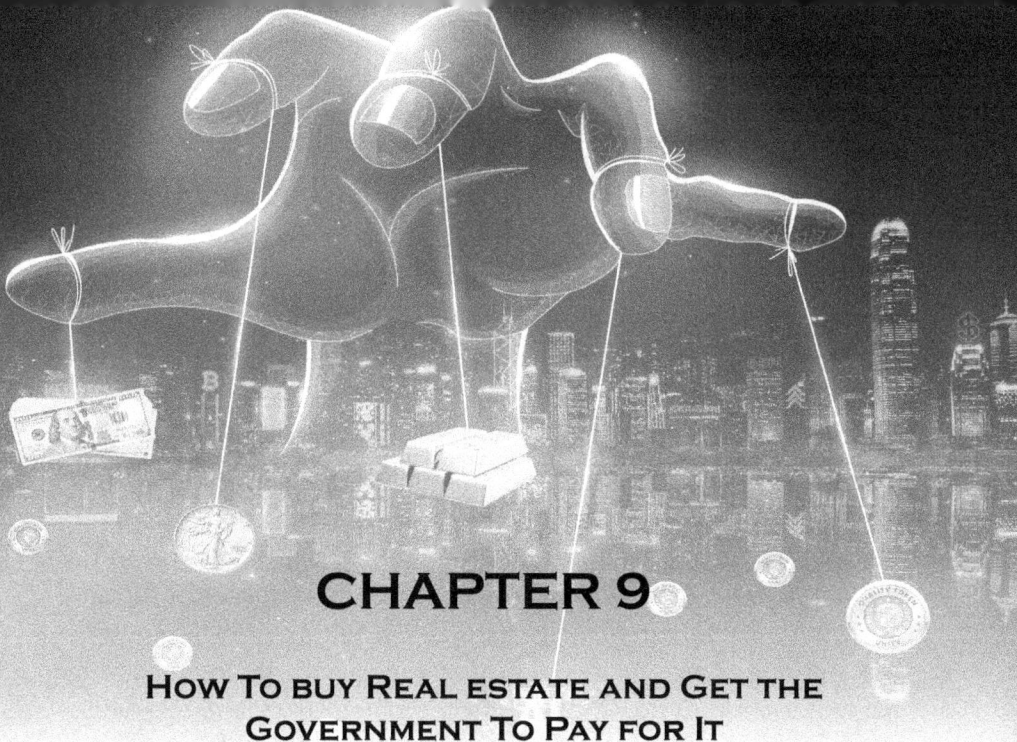

CHAPTER 9

HOW TO BUY REAL ESTATE AND GET THE GOVERNMENT TO PAY FOR IT

Now is the perfect time to buy real estate! After any crash in the economy, the next trend of the market is up! If you are wise and do just the opposite of what everyone else is doing then you too can prosper. Every time people would panic and sell, I would buy. When the stock market crashed in 2008, I was primarily on the side-lines with cash in the bank. I started buying real estate in 1989, and my first interest rate was at 10.5%, can you believe that, 10.5%. My mortgage payment was around $1,040.00 per month. I bought a Veterans Administration (VA) Foreclosure property for about $78,000.00. The V A guaranteed the loan, and I was into my first home at the age of thirty-four. The Veterans Administration's Loan Guarantee Program, was the first government program I used outside of the military.

Because I was a Vietnam Era veteran, I was able to secure the loan. Otherwise, I would not have qualified for the mortgage. My "debt to income ratio" was too high (more on that later). The house was a three bedroom, two full bathroom, Rambler. A Rambler is a ranch style house with a full basement. The basement was as large as the upstairs but it was unfinished, with the furnace and hot water heater sitting in the middle of the floor. GOD blessed me and I'm pretty handy around a house, so I determined that I would finish the basement, by working on it in the evenings. At this time I did not have any kids and I was separated from my spouse, with a live-in lady friend. I would leave home for work around 6:00 a.m. and return around 4:00 p.m. I would have dinner and begin working on my basement around 5:00 p.m. The first thing I did was to draw-up my plan. I wanted to make the basement a full apartment. I designed it to have two bedrooms, a full kitchen, full bath and a huge living/family room. The first thing I did was to move the hot water heater and the furnace, from the middle of the floor into a utility room on the side wall. I also plumbed in the connections for a washer and dryer.

I shared that I was handy around the house. I spent 12 years in the military as an aircraft mechanic. After learning the system of an airplane, the systems of a home were just natural. My full time job at this point was working as an aircraft production controller. I sat in an eight by ten foot room with no windows, three telephone lines, and two radios, one of them very high frequency (vhf), so that I could monitor the airplane/control tower conversations. But, they were always on and the chatter was non-stop. The phones were always ringing and we had a hot line to the fire department. We had a board with a diagram of the flight-line on it, with little miniature airplanes, which we could move around. We were responsible for keeping track of the planes' locations and maintenance status' at all times. It was all mental work. If you have ever been mentally tired at the end of the day, then you know what I mean. We were in that little room with no windows and dim lights for eight hours a day. We relied on the flight line supervisors to be our eyes and ears to the outside world. We only knew whatever they told us and then we would have to visualize it. Let's just say, by the end of the day, I was ready to take that hammer and make some nails pay!

I would work on that basement for four hours every night. I broke a hole through the concrete floor to install the bathroom. It had not been roughed in during the construction of the house. I framed up the kitchen and the utility room at the same time as the bathroom and ran the plumbing for the clothes washer and the kitchen sink. I don't know if you know it or not, but you can get certified as the homeowner and do your own electrical work.

What electrical work can you do?

You must own and live in the property to do the following work on low voltage electrical installations (when there is no payment or reward):

- Remove and replace any of the following kinds of fittings, where the work does not involve work on any switchboard:
- Switches,
- Socket outlets,
- Permanent connection units,
- Light fittings,
- Batten holders,
- Cord grip lamp holders,
- Ceiling roses,
- Flexible cords connected to any permanent connection unit, ceiling rose, or cord grip lamp holder,
- Water heater switches,
- Thermostats,
- Elements.
- Remove and replace fuse links.
- Connect and disconnect fixed wired appliances.
- Relocate existing switches, socket outlets, and lighting outlets that are supplied with electricity by tough plastic sheathed cables.
- Install, extend, and alter sub-circuits (including submains), provided that:
- The person must not enter (whether personally, by holding any material or equipment, or otherwise) any enclosure where live active conductors are likely to be present; and
- The work is tested by a licensed worker, in accordance with NZS 3000, and the work is certified by that licensed worker in accordance with regulation 66, before being connected to a supply of electricity by such an inspector.

You must get the finished job checked and tested by a licensed electrical inspector. You cannot connect your work to the electricity supply yourself. The inspector will connect it, test it, and issue you a Certificate of Compliance if it complies with safety requirements.

Hanging drywall by yourself is no joke, but I got it done, by the Grace of GOD. Four months later and a lot of blood, sweat and tears and I was finished. I used what a friend of mine's called a cripple. It was a two by four piece of wood with a shorter piece of two by four nailed to it at one end. Without this item I could never have finished my project. It's like having three hands, or another person in the room with you. In a room with an eight foot high ceiling, it requires two pieces of dry wall, one set on top of the other. I would install the first piece just above the floor, I would set another eight feet by four feet piece of dry wall, four feet in the and above the bottom piece, then use my cripple to keep it in place. My hands were now free and I would begin the installation process. I continued this process until the whole basement was finished.

The basement was now complete. Hallelujah! Praise the LORD! Right at that time, a blessing happened in my life. My girlfriend's friend wanted to move from Ohio to the Washington D.C. area. My basement was empty and ready, and she moved-in, paying $500.00 per month. Remember that my mortgage was around $1000.00 per month. I found myself with a $500.00 dollar per month positive cash flow. I shared this with my tax preparer, and he said brother, "if you don't do something Uncle Sugar, Sugar is going to eat you alive!" Single with no dependents is not a good filing status, when it comes to filing taxes in the United States of America. So, I excitedly asked him what I could do!

"Buy more real estate," was his reply! And so it began.

I needed more tax deductions and real estate was and still is one of the best tax deductions you can take. Right about this time in the early 1990's, there was a downturn in the real estate markets. Interest rates were lowered and the majority of people in the D.C area went upside down in their mortgages. It was a bad time for homeowners but a great time for real estate investors. Every Friday after work and on my way home, I would stop by the local Century 21 Real Estate office and pick up a copy of the VA Foreclosure Listing, for Maryland, Virginia and D.C. So every weekend, instead of going shopping at the mall, I would go shopping for houses. I didn't have GPS (Global Positioning Satellites) in those days, so a grabbed my copy of the street map guide by address, and got to work!

***If you managed to get this far in my book, your persistence will now be rewarded. For what I'm about to share with you will change your life forever. This secret I'm about to share with you revolutionized my thinking about buying real estate. I don't know of anyone else who is using this specific technique, and if they are they are not telling. ***

How did I get the Government to finance my real estate deals? Most of you may or may not be familiar with the federal government's Low Income Housing Program, now called the Affordable Housing Program. It's a program that helps families with low incomes to find affordable housing. The families who are eligible for this assistance under the program are issued, vouchers. At one time it was called the Section 8 program, and carried a negative connotation. Landlords working in this area were called slumlords. Many would be investors were turned off to this sector, just because of the name of the program. Remember the name of the program is the Low Income Housing Program. There are thousands of families out there where both the husband and wife are working but their combined incomes still left them below the poverty line. They are not terrible tenants who are going to destroy your property, and bring down the value of the neighborhood. They are hard-working citizens just like you and I. They pay their rent on time, maintain the property, and live in middle class neighborhoods. Here is the secret that you have been waiting for. Each eligible family is issued a voucher from the program with a guaranteed amount of assistance printed on the voucher. Once the recipient signed that voucher over to you, they could not change their mind and go with another landlord for one year. The bank also recognizes the voucher as income to you, so it changes your debt to income ratio!

(Debt to income Ratio: Debt-to-income ratio is abbreviated DTI, it is the percentage of your monthly gross income that goes toward paying debts. Your DTI can include principal, taxes, fees, and insurance premiums. When you go to the bank or mortgage company to get a loan they will be especially interested in this number.

So, you can easily qualify for a loan! Key to success: I would find the tenant before I bought the property! Sheer Genius! The rent was guaranteed for one year by the government, and they paid me the first month's rent, and a security deposit of one month's rent when the tenant would move in. My first mortgage payment was not due for thirty days after I closed on the property, so I had 30 days to do any repairs that were needed, and to get the property inspected and approved by the Housing Authority. The tenant would tell me where they wanted to live, and show me their voucher. I would shop for and find a house for sale in the neighborhood where they wanted to live. Once I had found the property and they agreed to rent it, they would sign their voucher's over to me. I would then take the voucher to the bank and get qualified for the loan. I would then purchase the property (the voucher amount always covered the mortgage with positive cash flow of $200.00 to $500.00 per month, after PITI = Principal, Interest, Taxes and Insurance), complete any repairs, get the property inspected, collect the first month's rent and the security deposit, and the tenant would move in. Win! Win! Win! As a real estate investor, I did not spend one day without a tenant, when I made my purchases, and because I was fair with my tenants they were long term renters. Some of them went on to own their own homes. Another real plus of this system is the fact that the tenants can become homeowners through this program if they qualify.

1   Eligible borrowers under this program are Section 8 voucher holders who have been approved by their local Public Housing Authority to participate in this program. This approval process includes assessments by counseling and credit services that will determine whether applicants are ready to purchase a home.

2   Eligible borrowers must be first-time homebuyers or cooperative members who meet minimum credit, income and employment standards. In addition, people who have owned homes before may also qualify for a loan under this program if they plan to purchase a home located in areas targeted for revitalization.

3   First-time homebuyers are those who have never purchased a home before or have not had an ownership interest in a principal residence for the past three years.

4   An applicant's annual, before-tax household income must not exceed the statewide income limits. This limit varies by state.

I repeated this process over and over again until 2004, by which time I had amassed ten single family houses and a four unit apartment building in the Maryland, Virginia, and Washington D.C. metro area.

I controlled those properties until 2006, when I sold them getting out of the market before the crash of 2008.

I BEAT THE GAME AND YOU CAN TOO!

CHAPTER 10

BEATING THE GAME

To beat the "Money Game" you must become a student of the game. That's how I did it! Information and hard work were my keys to success! I followed my mother's advice and outperformed everyone I worked with. I did not have to be the smartest or the brightest in the group, but I was always 100% the best that I could be. I consistently worked up to my potential. If the requirements for accomplishing the task were beyond my skill level, I did not hesitate to say so; but I would immediately do my research to find out the answer.

Once I had the appropriate information, then I was prepared to undertake the challenge. After I found this out, no challenge was too great. There was no hurdle I could not get over! The acquisition of knowledge became my passion. I would read, study, and listen to others to gain every ounce of information that was available. The whole universe became my teacher. I saw value in everything and everyone. The truth is, we are all made up of the same stuff, atoms (atom = Adam). I was not too proud to say to a client, "I don't know, but I will find out and get back with you". The next day I would follow-up and give them their answer. I learned the language of the industries or cultures where ever I journeyed. The Holy Scriptures are, and were my constant companions along every step of my journey. They can and will guide you to all truth. Read the scriptures for yourself. Don't just listen to other people and accept what they have to say about the scriptures.

Pray for wisdom and understanding; (ask and it shall be given, seek and you shall find, knock and the door will be opened unto you).

TAKE RESPONSIBILITY

I have always held positions of responsibility. When I was 19 years old in the military, I was already an Assistant Crew Chief on the B-52 aircraft. By age 20, I was in Thailand, and the youngest B-52 Crew Chief on the Flight-line. The lives of those air crew members were in my hands. If I did my job improperly, took shortcuts, or just plain didn't care, those crew members would end up dead, not from combat but from my negligence. It's the same with your finances, if you are lazy, take shortcuts, or just plain don't care about them (your finances), they will end-up dead on the "battle field of life". Take personal responsibility for your finances, because no one else will!

Prepare yourself to play and to win the "Money Game". Educate yourself, attend seminars, listen to learned people, and read everything you can about the subject. Reach out and get a mentor or a financial coach. Don't go it alone! Networking is the key! It's an old adage, "don't put all your eggs in one basket," but it's true and still applies to today's markets. Avoid debt at all cost! (But remember there is good debt and bad debt.) Some experts will tell you not to worry about debt. This may be true in the short term, but in the long haul "if you do not master debt, debt will master you". There are some fundamental principles that you must learn about money. They hold true no matter how poor or how wealthy you are. Leaders of countries, celebrities, star athletes, lottery winners, college professors, mentors, coaches, teachers, your parents and friends have all fallen victims to debt. The top one percent of the world's population use debt as a tool to manipulate nations, governments and individuals. If you are lazy and don't care about your financial future, just apply for your "MASTER" card, spend, spend, spend, and die a "Slave" in debt, leaving that debt as your legacy.

Just as in a game of chess, you must be strategic in your approach to the "Money Game." Invest in mutual funds, individual stocks and bonds, and 401k/IRA accounts! Purchase real estate, and own a small business to minimize taxes. You must incorporate yourself! Keep more of the money you have already earned. Budget and always know your F.I.N.

Multiple streams of income is the secret!

Take a balanced approached to life. Do whatever you please, the world belongs to you, but do it in moderation. Take care of your health. All the money in the world does not mean a thing if you are incapacitated in a hospital or nursing home, paying every dime of your savings to a doctor or medical facility; estranged from your friends and family, because of your ruthless approach to gaining wealth (Love people and use money, don't love money and use people). Eat a healthy diet. No! Don't go on a diet. Always eat healthy food, as much as possible, every day. Stay away from chemicals and refined sugar. Enjoy the journey, love all your friends and family. True prosperity comes in many different forms. Many people (actors, athletes, stock brokers, high government officials, religious leaders) with lots of money, take their own lives daily. Remember Wealth without Health is pointless.

Learn the local language

Even though it was outside of my degree field, I became a student of the financial services industry. I was licensed to sell, life and health insurance, property and casualty insurance, long term care insurance, disability insurance, and more. I was a Series 6 and 63 (A securities license entitling the holder to register as a limited representative and sell mutual funds, variable annuities and insurance premiums) licensed stock broker, selling mutual funds, and variable annuities. I was also a licensed Series 26, Principal (A securities license entitling the holder to register as a limited principal who supervises and manages sales activities for investment companies and annuities. The multiple choice exam is administered by Financial Industry Regulatory Authority (FINRA), previously known as the National Association of Security Dealers (NASD). I did not get a Real Estate license, nor did I want one, because the license places too many restrictions on the agents, and brokers are just more middlemen. Not having to worry about all those commissions, allowed the sellers to profit more from their transactions.

Therefore, they were more willing to sell their real estate to me, with outstanding terms. It was a win, win situation for everyone involved. That is where networking comes into play. Team-up with someone who has knowledge and expertise outside of your area of knowledge. Use these experts to free yourself from doing unprofitable things. Don't get bogged down in paperwork and trivial mtasks. Hire these things out.

Discover your gift. Each and every one of us has been given a gift from the Creator. Find your purpose in life and embrace it. Don't worry, if GOD has purposed it, then HE will provision it. The means to fulfill your divine purpose will always come to you, sometimes from unlikely sources. It is the law of attraction. Likewise, if you choose to live your life outside of the will of the Creator, you will expose yourself to lack and poverty. Poverty is not the will of the Creator for your life, but He will not violate your free choice/will. If we choose to violate the scriptural laws that govern the universe, then we open ourselves up to the consequences of violating those laws.

Fear and faith are opposite ends of the same spectrum, and cannot exist in the same space at the same time. No one knows where fear ends and faith begins or where faith ends and fear begins. Actually they are both the same thing. They're on a continuum. We're like the pendulum of a grandfather clock, swinging back and forth along this continuum. Today we're happy but tomorrow we are sad. The next day we're shouting with joy, and later that same day we find ourselves in the throes of despair. It's the same with taking on any task. It's a mind-set! At the start, we are sure we will complete the task in front of us. We're filled with confidence and believe we can conquer the world. But as time goes on fear and doubt begin to creep into our minds. Friends and relatives who have fears and doubts of their own start to give us advice. If and when we start to agree with them, we are doomed to failure. The power of agreement is another little known and understood scriptural principle. Because of this lack of knowledge and understanding we violate this principle all of the time. Our elders knew it and understood it. They tried to warn us but we would not listen. My grandmother would say, "be careful who you associate with"; "if you lay down with dogs you will get up with fleas"; "birds of a feather flock together"; "how can someone in the ditch with you give you advice on how to get out of the ditch."

19 Again I say unto you, That if two of you shall agree on earth as touching anything that they shall ask, it shall be done for them of my Father which is in heaven. 20 For where two or three are gathered together in my name, there am I in the midst of them. Matthew 18:19-20 King James Version (KJV)

Meditate on the Holy Scriptures, study them, read them, and pray for wisdom and understanding about them every day. Every motivational speaker, coach, trainer, professor or teacher I have ever met, knowingly or unknowingly, were quoting from the Holy Scriptures. You do not have to be "religious" for these scriptures to work in your life. You do not have to be "good" for these scriptures to work in your life. However, you do have to actively apply them. It is in the application of the scriptures that 98% of people fail. Successful men and women have adopted the principles contained in the scriptures, and use them daily. If you read and study their stories carefully you will see the truth. It's not always what they say, openly, it's the actions that they take and their inward belief systems. They set a goal, make a plan, write it down, repeat it daily, and never take no for an answer. Why do you think so many actors and actresses become wealthy? The human mind does not know the difference between fiction and reality. It will accept any programming we give it, both positive and negative! When you set a goal and determine to reach it no matter what happens in between, all the forces in the universe will combine to aid you in the accomplishing that goal.

"And you shall be like a tree planted by the rivers of water, that bringeth forth your fruit in your season; your leaf also shall not wither; and whatsoever you doeth shall prosper!" Psalm 1

Be an OVERCOMER:

7   He that overcometh shall inherit all things; and I will be his God, and he shall be my son.

8   But the fearful, and unbelieving, and the abominable, and murderers, and whoremongers, and sorcerers, and idolaters, and all liars, shall have their part in the lake which burneth with fire and brimstone: which is the second death. Rev. 21: 7-8

Don't Quit! There is a "Do It" inside of every don't-quit, and there is a Winner inside each and every one of you!

THE END

THE BEGINNING

CHAPTER 11

HOW I CONTINUE TO BE ON TOP OF THE GAME!

In July 2013 after living in retirement, in the Philippines, for the past nine years, I returned to the U.S. to check on a property I still owned there. It's a beautiful property located just 1 mile from the new National Harbor, on the Potomac River, near Washington D.C. It's situated on one and one quarter acres of land. This is one fantastic investment property that will just keep increasing in value. The potential for this property is unbelievable and will supply wealth for my family for generations to come. The property is zoned residential with a commercial variance. Right now, it can be subdivided into three additional building lots.I have four kids so each of them could have a home there if they are so inclined. Three of my kids moved with me to the Philippines just before I retired. It was not their choice but mine, so if they ever want to return and live in the United States they already have a place to build. The property is located within walking distance from the local elementary school, on a major Metro route, and 20 minutes' drive from the Washington Monument and other D.C. memorials. MGM Grand is building a $600 million casino just three miles from the property, with scheduled completion in the summer of 2016. Located just 4 miles off of Interstate 95 and the Capital Beltway 495, you can reach Richmond Virginia in under two hours, and New York City in about 4 hours.

I'm living in the Philippines, happily retired, in excellent health, sitting by my pool drinking mango shakes, and four-season juice (a "delightful blend" of pineapple, mango, orange and guava) daily. Life was good, tropical breezes, access to beautiful beaches, lush green mountains, and the capital city of Manila just two hours away by car. My family was in excellent health and all the medicinal plants (malungay, ampalya / bitter melon, Kalamansi, coconut, bayabas/ guava and mangosteen) were growing in my yard or at the local market. There are plants that are anti-inflammatory, anti-viral, anti-bacterial, anti-aging, anti-oxidant, infection fighting, and more. I would like to give another shout out to Xango, another MLM company that opened my eyes about the health benefits of the mangosteen fruit, and added an additional income stream to my portfolio. Wealth without health is overrated. You can truly call mangosteen a miracle plant, and it grows right here in the Philippines. You can get it at the local market or pick the fruit and leaves right from the tree if it grows near you (the best part is the pericarp/rind so don't throw it away). This is truly a fruit that modern medicine doesn't want you to know about. Could life get any better than this? GOD had given me prosperity beyond my wildest dreams. All my needs, wants and desires were being fulfilled, yet I am not proud or selfish, just humbled by the blessings.

I was also giving back to the community. I have a teaching/ feeding ministry, Psalm 1 Victory Foundation Inc., which feeds 500 to 600 indigent kids/families each year. We work closely with the Philippine Department of Social Welfare and Development (DSWD). They furnish us with the names of the deserving children/families and we conduct the feeding program. I would like to express thanks to all of our volunteers and donors. We love you and appreciate all that you do. GOD bless the workers at the DSWD, for their tireless efforts, helping the less fortunate members of our society.

How much better can this get? I flew back to the U.S. in July 2013. I checked out my property in Maryland and headed down to Richmond Virginia, in August, to visit a friend and to look in on a property I have across from Hunter Holmes McGuire VA Medical Center. I bought this property from a Filipino couple (Ate Eve and Kuya Frank) for cash, in 2006. As I mentioned before, I was able to sell the majority of my properties and move out of the market before the 2008 crash. I did an exchange into this property. Well, of course, this couple remembered me. If someone bought your home for cash you would remember them also. In fact, we became friends and I was going to visit them at their new home for lunch.

After finishing lunch and catching up on the past few years, we sat down to have a cup of tea. Their daughter Eloise and son in-law Gordon came in and said there was someone they wanted me to meet. I asked who and where was this person? Welcome to the twenty-first century and modern technology. He told me that the gentleman's name was Chuck and that we were going to Skype with him. He went on to share that he had discussed with Chuck, that I had been in Network/MultiLevel Marketing (MLM) before, and had retired early because of it.

Immediately, I told him that I was not interested in talking with Chuck, at all.My MLM days were behind me and that I had had a great run with it. I didn't know what a Skype was and that I would pass on the opportunity to talk with Chuck. Remember, I'd been out of the game for almost ten years and a lot had changed. He persisted in telling me how his son had joined the business and how much he loved it, and please just listen to Chuck and support his son. Yes, you guessed it, being a sucker for a cause, and wanting to support his son, I gave in. Lesson: $$ If you know you have a great cause or product, and someone says, no! Don't quit! They are just asking for more information on which to make a better decision. $$

We went downstairs, turned on the computer, opened Skype, and who came on the line, none other than Mr. Diamond Global Power Distributor himself, Chuck Williams (for you Network Marketing/ MLM fans, this is a three way call at its best). Gordon had already given Chuck a heads up, Chuck was ready, and I was now in front of him on the Skype. Chuck begin with some small talk and we became comfortable with each other. He asked if I had ever considered making money on-line. I replied yes, but it appeared to be a little bit complicated, time consuming and cost prohibitive. He agreed and we continued. His next question was if he could show me a way to save both time and money on the Internet, in a simple inexpensive way would I be interested? I said, yes of course I would be interested. Chuck introduced me to the SHOPPING SHERLOCK! I was amazed and I must admit quite skeptical! I asked a lot of questions and he answered them all. I still didn't fully understand how you could make money online without buying something or how you could give the Sherlock away for free and still make a profit. The concept was foreign to me and had not yet congealed in my mind. Chuck said good-by and said that we could talk again if I wanted to. I chatted awhile with Gordon and told him I didn't really understand Shopping Sherlock, but because he and his son was so excited about it that I would join and give it a year. I reached into my pocket, handed him $250.00 and said just sign me up. I said good-by to Ate Eve and Kuya Frank and departed for Maryland. About halfway back my phone rang and it was Gordon. He was a little hesitant at first to say what he wanted, but I said just let it out. He was so new, he did not know he could not enroll me with cash. He needed my credit card number, so I just gave it to him, along with the other information he needed to enroll me. Not bragging but Gordon had just landed the catch of a lifetime.

It's September 2013 and I've been enrolled in Shopping Sherlock since August and I have not done anything. I had forgotten that I had signed up and Gordon had not contacted me. (There is a lesson here: Follow-up with your people because you never know what is happening in their lives') Thank goodness for an active upline! Chuck had been sending me emails and keeping me informed about the company. We spoke again by phone and he said he really wanted to get Shopping Sherlock going in the Philippines and Asia, and that's why he was glad I was on the team. So, Chuck issued me a challenge ($$ it pays to listen to what people have to say and get a feel for what drives them $$). September would be a double bonus month for Shopping Sherlock. The CEO, Mr. Michael Wiedder, would pay $400.00 instead of the normal $200.00 to anyone making Power Distributor by the end of September 2013. It was already the 10th of September 2013, so Chuck asked if I thought I could do it. DO IT! That was our motto before during my A.L. William days. Of course I can do it, just get out of my way. From that moment, "The Game" was on again for me! I became a Power Distributor in 17 days, missing the bonus by just two days, but the money was not the important thing. The thrill of competing, and giving it my all, is what was important. I wanted to see if I could build a team again, take it to the TOP, and make everyone around me say, what happened? My activity got the attention of the CEO, Mr. Wiedder, and he spoke with me by phone.

Chuck and I have become great friends and spiritual brothers. Chuck introduced me to Mr. Pete Hamby, and wouldn't you know it, we bonded like we had known each other all of our lives. Pete and Chuck are friends, and mentors of mine for life. Pete and I got to know each other better at the Shopping Sherlock Convention, held at Green Valley Resort, Las Vegas Nevada, February 28th thru March 3, 2014. There were other legendary networkers at the convention, like the great Simon Brookes, from England. He's the only other Diamond Power Affiliate in Shopping Sherlock. Simon is the first Sherlock Affiliate to be paid $1 million and the company is only twenty five months old. The internationally known, Ms. Loral Langmeier, was also there, and spoke at the convention. Ms. Langmeier is a multi-millionaire in her own right, known as the "Millionaire Maker," is a part owner and affiliate with Shopping Sherlock. She's helping to expand Sherlock globally, in countries like South Africa. The Las Vegas Convention lit a spark in my teammates, like Power Affiliates Kyle Freeman and Carl Johnson, who are on the right side of my binary team; and the great Power Affiliates Art & Joy Wilson, with Tita Cook on my left side.

With their help and dedication we added over 100 people to the team by July 2014 and pushed to produce the first Global Power Affiliate in the Philippines. What an honor for "Team Victory!" We get to see the world and earn at the same time. My wife and I are off to London England in September 2014, for the first United Kingdom Sherlock Convention. Our reservations are already in for the U.S. Convention Cruise, to Jamaica and the Grand Cayman Islands, next March, 2015. We will be departing from Miami, Florida for the 5 night cruise. We will work very hard to win this cruise all expenses paid. The company has a promotion where if we qualify they will cover all the expenses of the trip. It doesn't get any better than that. My son will be accompanying us on the trip, and he is overjoyed, because this will be his first cruise. Shopping Sherlock is a family!

On Thursday, July 24, 2014, I kicked off my speaking tour. My son Willie Davis Jr., who is 12 years old, did the introduction and got things started, to a roaring round of applause, for his great diction.

What a great feeling as a father to know that your son will never have to work on a J.O.B! He's not shy or afraid of a crowd. He's a naturally gifted orator and speaks perfect English, even though he grew-up in the Philippines. My wonderful wife catered the outstanding food. She was the owner of Quality Catering, "The Caterer to the Stars," before retiring in 2003. She catered at the Warner Theater, MCI Center, and Constitution Hall, for such greats, as Robin Williams, Sinbad, Martin Lawrence, Kings of Comedy, Queens of Comedy, Bobby Womack, and the late Barry White and Bernie Mac, just to name a few. My youngest daughter has got the Sherlock bug and is working on building her team. She's just 18 years old but a senior at Holy Angel University, and was the ROTC's youngest Corps Commander in her junior year. By the time this book is published, she will be a Star Affiliate with Shopping Sherlock and on her way to building a great team. She is already dreaming about being a Diamond Global Power Affiliate. She's already written down her goals, and articulated her why. This is the first step in translating your dreams into reality. This is winning the money game at its best. When your whole family is happy, healthy and well balanced. The local newspaper, "Sun Star Pampanga," picked up the seminar titled "How Money Works," and published a great article, in the July 26, 2014 edition. If we are blessed/lucky, in our lifetime, opportunity will knock once upon our door. It is a rare occasion when we answer that knock, so most of us allow the opportunity to pass us by. I have been blessed to have opportunity to knock upon my door for the second time in my life. I took advantage of the first knock, and I plan to take full advantage of this second knock, and take as many people with me as possible! Don't allow doubt, fear and unbelief to chain you to a life of poverty. Live your life with passion knowing that you are on this planet for a purpose. "Death is not an ending but a beginning." Embrace your life, be a risk taker and live life to its fullest.

Shopping Sherlock has allowed me to come out of retirement, and to be "On Top of the Game" once again. If you're tired of the rat race, spinning your wheels and going nowhere, then this is the place for you. The market crash of 2008 was devastating to the world economies. People all over the world lost their savings, investments, pensions, retirement programs, homes and dreams. Get your millions back! Shopping Sherlock will be a billion dollar "Legacy" company. And I want to leave a LEGACY to my family! I know you do too!

ACKNOWLEDGMENT

I would like to take this opportunity to express my heartfelt appreciation and gratitude to all the individuals who have contributed to the completion of this new chapter. Without their unwavering support, dedication, and expertise, this project would not have been possible. First and foremost, I extend my deepest gratitude to Dr. Byron Nelson, Brandon Ivey, Dr. Lloyd Charles, Henry Bayubay, Miriam Baking, Ryanne Sugue, Uncle James, Ms. Marnita, Sister Wendy, Sister Rowena (Who has given me strength by being strong!) and Oscar and Wendy Villalobos. My Men's Bible Study Group: Dominic, Junie, Victor, Cortez, Joseph, Kelechi, Joey, and Rashmi. Also, our Faith-Driven Entrepreneur group: Sisters Joy, Faith, Ruby, Carol, Doctor Q, Bambi, and Brother Dominic. Their invaluable contributions have enriched this new chapter beyond measure. Dr. Byron Nelson, who was introduced to me by Mr. Brandon Ivey, has played an instrumental role in shaping its content, offering profound insights, and sharing his expertise and motivation. His passion for life has been truly inspiring, and his commitment to excellence is evident in every line. He helped me find my Voice again. I would also like to express my gratitude to the entire team of researchers, scholars, and professionals who have generously shared their knowledge, time, and expertise. Their collective efforts have made this new chapter a comprehensive and authoritative resource. Their meticulous attention to detail, thorough research, and insightful perspectives have greatly enriched the content and ensured its accuracy. I extend my thanks to the individuals who provided guidance, feedback, and valuable suggestions throughout the development of this project. Their constructive criticism and thoughtful input have significantly contributed to the refinement of the new chapter. Their willingness to share their expertise and engage in meaningful discussions have been instrumental in shaping its overall quality. Mr. Matthew Sparks, Ms. Kate Johnson, and Mr. Matthew C. Horne. Furthermore, I would like to acknowledge the support and encouragement of my family, friends, and colleagues. Their unwavering belief in my abilities and their continuous encouragement have provided me with the motivation and strength to pursue this project. Their presence throughout this journey has been a constant source of inspiration.

Finally, I would like to express my gratitude to the readers who will engage with this new chapter. Thank you for your interest in education about finances, cryptocurrency, NFTs, and the Metaverse. It is what motivated me to re-release my book and write a new chapter.

In conclusion, this new chapter is a gift of LOVE. I am deeply grateful to each one of the contributors for their unwavering support, expertise, and commitment. It is my sincere hope that this new chapter will serve as a valuable resource and inspire further advancement in your journey to "Financial Freedom".

Thank you all.

Sincerely,

WILLIE L. DAVIS SR.

CHAPTER 12

HOW I CONTINUE TO BE ON TOP OF THE GAME!

Part 2

So, you have read the book, studied the principles, determined where you are at in life, set your financial goals, wrote down your plans, prepared for emergencies or not, got an income (JOB), you are living month to month, paycheck to paycheck, and now you are ready to start your journey. You are now, "Ready for the Money Game!!" **STOP!**

No, you are not!

This is where 99% of the people go off the track to **Wealth** and end up on the financial tracks of mediocrity! They bought into the "Big LIE!" Go to School, get a good education, find a good JOB, work hard for 40 years, then get the Gold Watch!!! You are now too old and sick to travel and enjoy yourself. All your savings are going to hospitals and doctors, and your Health Insurance is nonexistent. Your grown kids are in the basement, and the State government is telling you, you must sell everything you own and move into a retirement facility before they can help you!!

Riches are not Wealth! And most people will not even be "**rich**". "Will you be a "One Percenter"? **One percent of the world population controls 99% of the wealth.**

Education is the key! Not a degree in "Basket Weaving 101", or a PhD in Statistics! You must obtain "Financial Literacy"!

Level UP

If you want to be better, you must be willing to stretch yourself. You can tell where you are **financially** in life, just by following these three steps. Here we go. Step 1. Take the incomes of your five closest friends. Step 2. Add them together. Step 3. Now, divide the total by five (5). Now you know why you are at your current level of income. If you want to be **"Financially Free"** you must level up. Set your **GOALS** then surround yourself with likeminded people, who can help you accomplish those goals. The "**Law of the Universe**" will come into play, and success will find you!

Saving your fiat currency in a bank account, company retirement plan, 401K, Certificate of Deposit (CD), etc. is not the answer. With the multitude of Bank Failures occurring Worldwide, as I am writing this chapter, (21 May 2023). All of my predictions/observations from 2014, when I first published, "How I Beat the Money Game", are happening, NOW!!!!

If "YOU" do not physically possess your Properties/Commodities, then they do not belong to YOU!!!

So here is the Big Question, "What Do I Do??"

When it comes to personal finances, being satisfied with your financial situation is often a matter of perspective and can depend on several factors, including income, expenses, debt, and savings. Some people may feel satisfied with their financial situation if they have a stable income, low debt, and a healthy savings account, while others may feel dissatisfied even if they have a high income and significant savings if they are struggling to make ends meet each month or have large amounts of debt.

It is important to remember that personal finances are a journey and not a destination. Financial satisfaction is something that can be achieved and maintained over time with careful planning and smart financial decisions. Here are some tips to help you become more satisfied with your financial situation:

1   Set financial goals: Having specific financial goals in mind can help you focus your efforts and make it easier to measure your progress. Your goals might include paying off debt, building an emergency fund, saving for retirement, or buying a home. Write down your goals, determine what you need to do to achieve them, and track your progress regularly.

2   Create a budget: Creating and sticking to a budget is one of the most effective ways to take control of your finances. Determine how much you earn each month and how much you spend in each category, such as housing, food, transportation, and entertainment. Make adjustments as needed to ensure that you are living within your means and are on track to reach your financial goals.

3   Pay off debt: Debt can be a significant source of financial stress, so it's important to pay it off as soon as possible. Prioritize paying off high-interest debt, such as credit card balances, and make extra payments whenever you can. Consider debt consolidation or a debt management plan if you are struggling to keep up with your payments.

4   Build an emergency fund: Having a solid emergency fund can help you weather financial storms, such as job loss or unexpected expenses. Aim to save three to six months' worth of living expenses in a separate savings account that you can access in an emergency.

5   Invest in your future: In addition to saving for emergencies, it is also important to save for the future. Consider investing in a retirement plan, such as a 401(k) or an individual retirement account (IRA), or a taxable investment account. Make regular contributions to these accounts and consider working with a financial advisor if you need help choosing the right investment options for your needs.

6   Live within your means: Living within your means is the key to financial satisfaction. Avoid lifestyle inflation and resist the temptation to keep up with the Joneses. Focus on spending on

the things that are important to you, such as experiences with loved ones or personal growth opportunities, rather than on keeping up appearances.

7   Seek help when needed: If you are struggling with your finances, don't be afraid to seek help. Consider working with a financial advisor or credit counselor to get a better handle on your debt, create a budget, or plan for retirement. Joining a support group or connecting with a financial mentor can also provide valuable resources and guidance.

By following these tips and making smart financial decisions, you can work toward financial satisfaction and peace of mind. Remember that personal finances are a journey and making mistakes along the way is okay. The key is to learn from those mistakes and continue moving forward.

Financial satisfaction is not a one-time achievement, but rather a continuous process of learning.

Education Trumps Fear Every Time

The financial world has undergone a major transformation in the past few decades, with the rise of digital currencies and precious metals becoming increasingly prominent as investment options. While these new avenues for investment can be exciting and offer great potential for growth, they can also be intimidating and overwhelming for many people. This is where education comes in. The more you know about a particular investment, the less fear and anxiety you will have about it.

Let us start with precious metals. Precious metals, such as gold and silver, have been used as a store of value for thousands of years. They have been a popular form of investment for just as long, with many people turning to them as a safe- haven during times of economic uncertainty. When you educate yourself about precious metals, you will learn that they offer a tangible asset that is not tied to any particular fiat currency or government. They are also finite in supply, meaning that they can hold their value even when other investments are losing ground.

One of the most important things to understand about investing in precious metals is that they tend to move in the opposite direction of the stock market. This means that when the stock market is performing poorly, precious metals may be performing well, and vice versa. This makes them a good hedge against economic instability and a useful addition to any investment portfolio.

The world of digital currencies, also known as cryptocurrencies, is a relatively new one. Cryptocurrencies are digital or virtual tokens that use cryptography to secure and verify transactions. The first and most well-known cryptocurrency is Bitcoin, but there are now hundreds of different cryptocurrencies available for investment.

Investing in cryptocurrencies can be a high-risk, high-reward proposition. Because cryptocurrencies are decentralized and not tied to any government or central authority, their value is based purely on supply and demand in the market. This can make them volatile, with rapid price swings happening in a matter of days or even hours.

However, despite the risks, investing in cryptocurrencies can also offer great potential for growth. Some investors have seen returns of several thousand percent in just a few short years. It is important to remember, though, that investing in cryptocurrencies is not for the faint of heart. It requires a willingness to accept high levels of risk in exchange for the potential for high rewards.

Whether you are considering investing in precious metals or cryptocurrencies, the key to reducing fear and anxiety is education. By learning more about these investment options, you will gain a deeper understanding of the risks and potential rewards involved. This will give you the confidence you need to make informed investment decisions and pursue your financial goals with greater ease. Remember, education trumps fear every time, and the more you know about your investments, the better equipped you will be to make decisions that will lead to success.

To get to where you want to go, you must know where you are at. What is your current location/status? If you do not know that you are trapped, you will never try to escape.

Living on a Modern-Day Financial Plantation

Living on a modern-day financial plantation refers to a system where individuals and communities are trapped in a cycle of debt and poverty, with limited access to wealth and financial stability. This system is perpetuated by a combination of factors, including systemic discrimination, unequal access to education and job opportunities, and predatory lending practices. Let us explore how this financial plantation system operates and its effects on those trapped within it.

One of the key ways in which the modern-day financial plantation operates is through predatory lending practices. These practices involve the targeting of individuals and communities with high-interest loans, often with hidden fees and terms that trap borrowers in a cycle of debt. For example, payday loans and highinterest credit cards are marketed toward individuals with low incomes or poor credit and are designed to keep them in debt for long periods of time. This not only keeps these individuals and communities in a state of financial instability, but it also profits the lenders and perpetuates the cycle of poverty.

Another factor that contributes to the modern-day financial plantation is systemic discrimination. This includes discrimination in areas such as housing, employment, and education, which leads to unequal access to wealth-building opportunities and financial stability. For example, redlining, the practice of denying or limiting loans or insurance to residents of certain neighborhoods, often based on race or ethnicity, has a lasting impact on communities of color and their ability to build wealth. Similarly, unequal access to quality education and job opportunities, often based on race and socio-economic status, contributes to the cycle of poverty and financial instability.

The effects of living on a modern-day financial plantation are far-reaching and devastating. It traps individuals and communities in a cycle of debt, preventing them from achieving financial stability and independence. This lack of stability can have a significant impact on mental health and overall well-being, as individuals are constantly worried about paying bills and avoiding debt. It also perpetuates the cycle of poverty, as individuals are unable to build wealth and pass it on to future generations.

Living on a modern-day financial plantation is a reality for many individuals and communities in the United States and around the world. It operates through predatory lending practices and systemic discrimination, trapping individuals and communities in a cycle of debt and poverty. Addressing these issues requires systemic changes, including stronger consumer protections and greater access to wealth-building opportunities for marginalized communities. Only then can we begin to break the cycle of poverty and financial instability and build a more equitable and just society.

How to Escape the Modern-day
Financial   Plantation
The Solution!!

The modern-day financial plantation is a term used to describe the cycle of debt, poverty, and limited financial options that trap many individuals and communities. This financial system can seem like a never-ending cycle, with people struggling to make ends meet, relying on high-interest loans, and living paycheck to paycheck. However, it is possible to escape this cycle, and it starts with education and empowerment. The first step towards financial freedom is education. Financial literacy is the cornerstone of successful money management. Individuals must understand basic financial concepts such as budgeting, saving, investing, and debt management. This knowledge will help them make informed decisions about their money and avoid financial traps such as payday loans, high-interest credit card debt, and predatory lending practices. There are many resources available, including online classes, books, and workshops that can help individuals develop the skills they need to manage their money.

The second step is to create a budget. A budget is a plan for how to use your money, and it is the foundation of good money management. When creating a budget, individuals should start by listing all their income and expenses, and then look for areas where they can cut back on spending. By creating a budget and sticking to it, individuals can take control of their finances, reduce their debt, and start saving for the future.

The third step is to save. Building an emergency fund is critical for financial stability. An emergency fund is a savings account that is used to cover unexpected expenses, such as car repairs, medical bills, or job loss. It is recommended to aim for an emergency fund that covers three to six months of living expenses. In addition to an emergency fund, individuals should also save for long-term goals, such as retirement, a down payment on a house, or a child's education.

The fourth step is to invest. Investing is a way to grow wealth over time, and it is an important component of a well-rounded financial plan. There are many different types of investments, including stocks, bonds, real estate, and mutual funds, and individuals should choose the options that are right for their financial goals and risk tolerance. Working with a financial advisor can help individuals make informed investment decisions and create a diversified portfolio.

The modern-day financial plantation can be a difficult cycle to break, but it is possible. By educating themselves, creating a budget, saving, and investing, individuals can take control of their finances and build a better future. The key is to start small and make incremental changes, building momentum over time.

With hard work, dedication, and the right tools, anyone can escape the modernday financial plantation and secure their financial future.

DECISIONS, DECISIONS, DECISIONS
Gold and Silver

Why Buy Gold and Silver?

There are many reasons why you should own physical gold and silver as a part of your investment strategy. Unlike paper investments like stocks, bonds, mutual funds, and fiat currencies, you can take physical possession of your gold and silver. Precious metals like gold and silver can be owned and held in your custody. In today's environment, having your metals close at hand is a big deal. Fiat currencies around the world are on the brink of collapse and the central banks are printing them like crazy. Currently, the National Debt of the United States of America is over Thirty-one Trillion Dollars ($31,497,240.345,231.00). By the time this book is published, the debt could be more than Thirty-two Trillion Dollars. The debt per U.S. citizen is $94,173.00 and over $246,866.00 per U.S. taxpayer. https://www.usdebtclock.org/ This is a debt that can never be repaid. The politicians know this, but they continue to spend, and spend, with little regard for the people. Historically, gold and silver have performed very well when the stock market crashes or corrects. They are considered to be safe haven assets and owning them can reduce your risk during uncertain times.

GOLD AND SILVER ARE NOT THE ONLY PRECIOUS METALS

Platinum, Rhodium, and Palladium are also rare precious metals that are listed and traded. The following is a list of benefits and a breakdown of each of these metals.

Gold

Gold has been a highly sought-after symbol of wealth since the beginning of recorded history. Because it is malleable, resistant to corrosion, and conducts electricity, gold has many practical uses, in several industries. But it is mainly used as a store of value. Gold is considered an excellent long-term investment and offers benefits those other investments cannot.

According to Alan Greenspan – "Gold, unlike all other commodities, is a currency, and the major thrust in the demand for gold is not for jewelry. It's not for anything other than an escape from what is perceived to be a fiat money system, paper money that seems to be deteriorating."

Silver

Silver is perhaps the oldest mass-produced form of coinage, in the world. Silver has been used as a coinage metal since the times of the Greeks. The Spanish reportedly took over 16,000 tons of silver out of South America, between 1500 and 1650 AD. Silver is a soft, white, lustrous metal, and exhibits the highest electrical conductivity, of any metal. With its collectability and its many uses as an industrial metal, jewelry, and coinage. These multiple demands make silver a very desirable commodity. Silver is used in electric cars, solar panels, cell phones, computers, and the list goes on and on.

Platinum, Rhodium, and Palladium

Platinum, Palladium, and Rhodium are rare precious metals used in many of the same ways as gold and silver. Rhodium is a precious silver-white metal, with a high reflectivity for light. It is not corroded or tarnished by the atmosphere at room temperature. Platinum and palladium are both known for their excellent catalytic properties and are used heavily in the automobile industry, as well as in the manufacturing of jewelry and numerous other items.

What Is In It For Me?

Most people want to know, "What is in this investment for me"? What you invest your money in is nobody's business but your own. When you purchase gold and silver for delivery to your home, your purchases are entirely private. Having gold and silver in your possession means no government or financial institution is involved in your financial decisions. This was a biggie for me. I love my privacy!! China is leading the way with "Social Credit" scoring. Cameras are on every corner, a cell phone in every hand, dash cams, nanny cams, and buttonhole cameras… make privacy more important than ever.

Supply & Demand

The demand for physical gold and silver from central banks, governments, financial institutions, big industry, and the general public is increasing at levels never seen before. This creates a ready market where your coins can be easily sold or traded. The demand for the safety and security offered by physical precious metals will only continue to rise as political and economic uncertainty continues to grow. As technology continues to evolve, the need for gold and silver as industrial metals will also continue to increase. Gold and silver miners appear to be avoiding new projects. The global economic picture is one of uncertainty, and gold and silver prices could skyrocket in the near future.

Liquidity

Gold and silver coins are valued worldwide and can be sold or traded almost anywhere, instantly. Gold and silver are some of the most liquid assets you can own. Owning physical metals gives you peace of mind. Having them in your possession allows you to have something of value at your fingertips and gives you the ability to sell your gold and silver without having to go through centralized systems filled with hurdles and other challenges.

Diversification

Do not put all your eggs in one basket. This should be common sense, but common sense is not common. Spread your investments around. This is necessary to achieve a balanced investment portfolio. Diversifying your assets among stocks, bonds, cash, and precious metals is a sound strategy. In fact, precious metals have outperformed every major investment index over the same period. Gold and silver in your portfolio act as a hedge against currency weakness, political instability, economic collapse, and market volatility. These metals are also means of wealth storage over centuries and, thus, are better in many ways than stocks and bonds. These metals also maintain their purchasing power worldwide over the long term.

Cost of Money

Most of us recognize that the buying power of fiat currency has dramatically decreased over time. Gold and silver can be powerful allies against inflation. As the Federal Reserve and Central banks around the world continue to raise rates and print more paper/digital currency, people will flock to precious metals. The Federal Reserve raised the federal funds rate seven times in 2022, with more on the way for 2023. To preserve your purchasing power, gold, and silver are a rather good move.

Growth Potential

Gold and silver cannot be printed or created on a computer – they are finite resources. Because the amount of gold and silver is limited, they can grow in value. In the past, gold and silver have provided significant returns to investors. Today, the prices of gold and silver are at relatively low levels. Precious metals are a desirable investment opportunity for many people because compared to savings accounts and other low-yielding investments, there can be an opportunity for greater growth potential.

Precious Metals Fall Into Different Categories - Bullion, Semi-Numismatic, Numismatic & Junk Silver –

When investing in precious metals, you have three primary choices, bullion, seminumismatic and numismatic. There are unique benefits to all three types, depending on your goals, but there are some fundamental differences between them:

Bullion coins and bars are usually made from gold and silver and may also be available in platinum and palladium. They are generally minted in weights that are fractions of one troy ounce to fit a variety of budgets.

Bullion products command the lowest premium in the marketplace as compared to the spot price of the underlying precious metal. Bullion coins will rarely ever have a value much greater than the current spot price of the metal from which they are struck. Bullion products are also produced in much higher quantities when compared to either Numismatic or Semi-Numismatic coins. Their abundance and consistent availability in the market also contribute to the lower prices associated with bullion products.

Numismatic coins are those minted prior to 1933. Numismatic coins have value beyond the materials they are made from. This numismatic or collectible value may be due to a coin's age, condition, rarity, design, historical significance or most often a combination of these factors. Numismatic coins will often receive a condition 'grade' from a professional coin grading service. But, just like a bullion coin, numismatic coins are also valued for the content of their precious metal. Numismatic coins carry the highest premiums of all coins.

Because their value does not solely rely on their metal content, many investors are attracted to the opportunity to have more than one factor determining the value of their coins.

Semi-numismatic coins are coins that share both bullion and numismatic traits. Generally, they are bullion coins that have a limited mintage (total number produced) and are attractive to collectors due to their design, special features, form factor, or overall series popularity.

During its production run at the mint, a semi-numismatic coin can be purchased at a reasonable premium over the spot price of the metal. It might be slightly higher than a pure bullion coin, but not by too much. However, once the production run is over and the mint sells out of inventory the premium over spot bumps up. As the inventory at dealers dwindles, the premium rises more.

Many investors and collectors believe that a semi-numismatic coin is the best of both worlds. It provides all the benefits of owning gold or silver bullion while providing the upside of investment appreciation independent of the metals' spot price.

Junk Silver

Ninety Percent (90%) Junk Silver Coins and Face Bags. Junk Silver Coins, also known as US 90% Silver Coins, generally refer to old US currency coins whose value is based on their silver bullion content. These are 90% silver coins minted by the US Government pre-1965 (half dollars, quarters, and dimes). These are the types of coins you would want to have on hand, as a means of survival, in case of a total collapse of the U.S. dollar.

How To Buy Precious Metals

The first thing you may want to do is to find a trusted source at a nearby location: Get to know your local coin dealer. Local coin shops have been around for almost as-long-as money itself. Once you start to search for them you will start seeing them everywhere. It is amazing how that works. Two of the most common places to purchase your metals are these local coin shops and online dealers. One of my favorite online sources is GoldSilver.com. https://www.goldsilver.com

They accept Bitcoin as one of their primary forms of payment. We will talk more about being able to use cryptocurrency as a payment vehicle later. Note: I sold Bitcoin and bought Silver when Bitcoin was at $65,000.00 USD per coin!!! A few months after that purchase the price of Bitcoin declined to below $17,000.00 per coin and has traded sideways ever since. So now I am dollar-costaveraging back into Bitcoin at $250.00 per week. Unlike most people who are crying gloom and doom, I want Bitcoin to stay low!! In less than 18 months I will have my one Bitcoin back, and I will have over 2,200 Silver Eagles in my possession. It does not get any better than that.

Tangible Holdings

Buying precious metals for physical possession allows you to store your metals however you choose – at home, in a safe, in a bank deposit box, under your mattress, in the backyard, and so on. You always have total control over your investment and complete access to your metals. That level of peace of mind is priceless, and can be a legacy for your family,

Precious Metals Self-Directed IRAs

If you already have your money in an Individual Retirement Account (IRA), you may want to consider, moving it to a Precious Metal Self-Directed IRA.Precious Metals IRAs combine the benefits of precious metals with the tax benefits of a government-approved retirement account. A variety of coins and bars from around the world are approved for a Precious Metals IRA. They can be stored safely in a precious metals depository until you decide to take distributions from your account. Storage can be inside of the U.S. or at an approved location Outside the Continental United States (OCONUS) if that is what you desire.

Other investment types can also be added to a Self-Directed Precious Metals IRA, such as stocks, mutual funds, real estate, mortgages, etc...

Deciding which way to invest should be based on your individual goals and circumstances. Some investors use Precious Metals IRAs for their retirement savings while also keeping additional metals stored at home or in a safe.

CURRENCY WARS: ARE WE WINNING?

We are at war, whether you know it or not. Foreign countries and the Elites are buying gold and silver.

If you want to be wealthy, **"determine where the wealthy are going, then get there before they do, or arrive at the same time".**

This chart is from GoldSilver. It shows the difference between the S&P 500 and Gold and Silver during the biggest declines in the stock markets since 1976. The next stock market crash is at hand. Be prepared!

Gold Performance During Stock Market Crashes   GOLDSILVER

Dates of S&P 500's Biggest Declines	S&P 500	Gold	Silver
Sep 21, 1976 - Mar 6, 1978	-19.4%	53.8%	15.2%
Nov 28, 1980 - Aug 12, 1982	-27.1%	-46.0%	-66.1%
Aug 25, 1987 - Dec 4, 1987	-33.5%	6.2%	-11.8%
Jul 16, 1990 - Oct 11, 1990	-19.9%	6.8%	-10.8%
Jul 17, 1998 - Aug 31, 1998	-19.3%	-5.0%	-9.5%
Mar 27, 2000 - Oct 9, 2002	-49.0%	12.4%	-14.4%
Oct 9, 2007 - Mar 9, 2009	-56.8%	25.5%	1.1%
May 10, 2011 - Oct 3, 2011	-19.0%	9.4%	-19.1%
Feb 19, 2020 - Mar 23, 2020	-33.9%	-4.9%	-31.8%
AVERAGE	-30.9%	6.5%	-16.4%

Cryptocurrency

Cryptocurrency has become one of the most talked-about and debated topics in recent years, with the market for digital currencies growing at an astonishing pace. With so many people jumping on the bandwagon and so much money being poured into the crypto market, it can be overwhelming to try to make sense of it all and determine the best way to get involved. However, by following a few key principles, you can effectively ride the wave of cryptocurrency and maximize your chances of success.

1.   **Educate yourself on the basics of cryptocurrency**

The first step to effectively riding the wave of cryptocurrency is to educate yourself on the basics of the technology and the market. Cryptocurrency is a digital or virtual currency that uses cryptography to secure and verify transactions as well as to control the creation of new units. The most well-known and widely used cryptocurrency is

Bitcoin, but there are many other cryptocurrencies that are gaining popularity, including Ethereum, Ripple, and Litecoin.

To better understand how cryptocurrency works, it is important to familiarize yourself with the underlying technology known as blockchain. Blockchain is a decentralized digital ledger that records transactions across a network of computers. It is secure and transparent, making it an ideal platform for digital currency transactions.

It is also important to understand the basics of cryptocurrency markets and trading. This includes understanding the various exchanges where you can buy and sell digital currencies, as well as the different types of orders you can place and the fees associated with trading. **I recommend Mr. Brandon Ivey's – 5-Day Challenge - https://ilcachallenge.com for the greatest Crypto education on the market today. Best of all the 5-day course is FREE to attend. Just click the link and enroll.**

2.   Determine your investment goals

Once you have a good understanding of the basics of cryptocurrency, the next step is to determine your investment goals. This will help you make informed decisions about the type of currency to invest in, the amount of money to invest, and the time horizon for your investment.

For example, if you are looking for a long-term investment, you may want to consider investing in a more established cryptocurrency like Bitcoin or Ethereum, which have a proven track record and a strong market presence. On the other hand, if you are looking for a short-term investment, you may want to consider investing in a newer cryptocurrency with a high potential for growth, but also a higher level of risk.

It is also important to consider your investment goals in terms of risk tolerance. Some people are willing to take on more risk in exchange for the potential for higher returns, while others prefer a more conservative approach with a lower risk of loss.

3. Diversify your portfolio

Diversification is an important principle of investing, and it is especially relevant when investing in cryptocurrency. This is because the crypto market is highly volatile, and the value of individual cryptocurrencies can fluctuate dramatically. By diversifying your portfolio, you can spread your risk and reduce the impact of market volatility on your investment.

For example, instead of investing all your money in one cryptocurrency, you could consider investing in a combination of different cryptocurrencies that have different risk-reward profiles. This might include a mix of established cryptocurrencies like Bitcoin and Ethereum, as well as newer and more speculative cryptocurrencies with high growth potential.

4. Stay Informed

The cryptocurrency market is constantly changing, with new developments and events affecting the value of digital currencies. To effectively ride the wave of cryptocurrency, it is important to stay informed and up to date on the latest news and trends in the market.

You can stay informed by following the news and social media accounts of the cryptocurrencies you are invested in, as well as monitoring forums and discussion boards dedicated to the crypto market. You can also subscribe to newsletters and join online communities to stay informed and connected with other investors.

5. Be patient and disciplined

Finally, it is important to be patient and disciplined when investing in cryptocurrency. Dollar-cost averaging (DCA) is a great strategy! In Dec 2022, BTC was trading sideways for around $16,000.00 to $17,000.00 per coin. Today, 23 May 2023, BTC is trading at $26,937.00 per coin. In addition, we are heading into a BTC halving in 2024. The halving is when the fees paid to the BTC miners are reduced.In the 2024 halving, the reward will drop from 6.25 BTC per block to 3.125 BTC. This will have a dramatic effect on the price of BTC.

6.   **Use a reputable exchange**

When investing in cryptocurrency, it is important to use a reputable exchange. A reputable exchange will have strong security measures in place to protect your funds and will also provide transparent pricing and good customer support.

It is also important to choose an exchange that is regulated, as this will provide you with greater protection and ensure that the exchange is operating in a legal and transparent manner.

7.   **Keep your investments secure**

Securing your investments is crucial in the world of cryptocurrency. This means keeping your private keys safe, as these are the keys that allow you to access and control your cryptocurrency holdings.

One of the best ways to keep your cryptos safe is by selecting the right wallet.

Some examples are:Exodus, Atomic, Divi, Klever, MetaMask, TronLink, Trust.

Hard Wallets include: Trezor and Ledger

For added protection and security: Crypto only Laptops and Secure Crypto only Cell Phones are also popular. They are kept off-line and only connected to the internet via ethernet cords using a VPN, when transacting. Never use WIFI with your crypto only devices.

What are NFTs and What Do They Mean To Me?

NFTs, or non-fungible tokens, have recently taken the world by storm, causing excitement and confusion in equal measure. Let us explore what NFTs are and what they mean to you as an individual.

At their core, NFTs are unique digital assets that exist on a blockchain. This means that each NFT has a unique identifier that distinguishes it from all other NFTs, and the ownership of an NFT is verified and recorded on the blockchain. This verification makes NFTs unique and valuable because it gives them scarcity, which is something that is often lacking in the digital world.

NFTs are most commonly used for buying, selling, and trading art, but they have a wide range of other potential uses, such as creating digital collectibles, managing digital identities, and even building decentralized apps. They are a tool that enables creators to retain ownership and control over their digital creations, something that has been difficult to achieve in the past.

To me, NFTs are a symbol of the shifting landscape of digital ownership and creativity. They represent a way to truly own and control something digital, and they give creators a way to monetize their work in a new and innovative way.

They are a reflection of the increasing importance of digital assets in our lives, and they provide a platform for artists, musicians, and other creatives to showcase their work and reach new audiences.

Furthermore, NFTs provide a new opportunity for collectors to invest in unique and valuable digital assets. They allow collectors to own a piece of something that is truly one-of-a-kind and that will retain its value over time. This is a new and exciting development, as traditional investments such as stocks and bonds are becoming increasingly difficult for average people to access.

NFTs are a fascinating development in the world of digital assets and creativity. They are a tool for creators to monetize their work, a platform for collectors to invest in unique digital assets, and a symbol of the shifting landscape of digital ownership. To me, they represent a new and exciting way to engage with digital art and creativity, and they have the potential to greatly impact the future of digital assets and ownership.

THE METAVERSE

The Metaverse refers to a collective virtual shared space, created by the convergence of virtually enhanced physical reality and physically persistent virtual reality, including the sum total of all virtual worlds, augmented reality, and the internet. In essence, the Metaverse is a virtual universe where individuals can interact and engage in a wide range of activities, both real and imagined.

As the Metaverse continues to grow and evolve, it is becoming increasingly important for individuals to have the skills and knowledge necessary to thrive in this new environment. In this article, we will discuss some of the key factors that are essential for survival in the Metaverse and provide some tips for how you can thrive in this exciting new world.

1   Understanding the Technology

One of the most important aspects of surviving in the Metaverse is having a solid understanding of the technology that makes it possible. This includes understanding the hardware and software platforms that are used to access and participate in the Metaverse, as well as the underlying principles of virtual reality and augmented reality.

It is also important to stay up-to-date on the latest advancements in technology as new and improved hardware and software are constantly being developed and released. Keeping up with the latest developments will help you to stay ahead of the curve and ensure that you have the skills and knowledge necessary to fully partici-pate in the Metaverse.

2   Building a Strong Network

In the Metaverse, just as in the physical world, building strong relationships and networks is the key to success. This means reaching out to other users, participating in virtual communities, and making connections with like-minded individuals.

By building a strong network in the Metaverse, you will have access to a wealth of information, resources, and support that can help you to succeed and thrive. Additionally, having a strong network will also help you to stay connected with others, even when you are not physically present in the Metaverse.

3   Developing a Unique Identity

In the Metaverse, your identity is an important aspect of your overall experience. It is important to create a unique and recognizable avatar that represents you and your personality. This can be achieved through customizing your avatar's appearance, clothing, and other visual elements.

Having a strong and recognizable identity in the Metaverse can help you to establish your reputation and increase your visibility among other users. It can also help you to build trust and credibility, which can be essential for success in this virtual world.

4   Finding Your Niche

One of the great things about the Metaverse is that there are endless opportunities for individuals to explore and find their niche. This can be achieved by participating in a variety of virtual activities, such as gaming, socializing, and even virtual work.

By finding your niche in the Metaverse, you can tap into your passions and interests and engage in activities that are truly meaningful and fulfilling. This can help you to find a sense of purpose and satisfaction in the Metaverse, which is essential for overall well-being and happiness.

5   Building Strong Virtual Communities

In the Metaverse, virtual communities play an important role in fostering connection and collaboration between individuals. These communities can be centered on shared interests, such as gaming or social activism, or they can be focused on specific geographic locations or cultures.

Building strong virtual communities can help you to stay connected with others, even when you are not physically present in the Metaverse. It can also provide you with a sense of belonging and help you to find support and guidance as you navigate this virtual world.

6   Staying Safe and Secure

As with any online environment, safety and security are essential for survival in the Metaverse. This means taking steps to protect your personal data.

How do I stay Safe and Secure in the Metaverse?

The Metaverse, being an immersive digital world, has its own set of security and privacy concerns. Here are some ways you can stay safe and secure in the Metaverse:

1 Use strong passwords: Use strong and unique passwords that are difficult to guess or crack. Enable two-factor authentication wherever possible to add an extra layer of security to your accounts.

2 Be cautious of phishing scams: Be cautious of emails or messages that ask you to provide sensitive information, such as passwords or financial details. Scammers may use the guise of official Metaverse organizations or avatars to trick you into revealing your information.

3 Be mindful of what you share: Be mindful of what personal information you share in the Metaverse, as it can be used for identity theft or other malicious purposes. This includes your name, address, email address, and financial information.

4 Keep your software up to date: Regularly update your Metaverse software, including your VR headset and any relevant apps, to ensure that you have the latest security patches and features.

5 Use trusted sources: Only download software and assets from trusted sources, and be cautious of downloading anything from unknown or untrusted sources as it may contain malware or other malicious content.

6 Use privacy settings: Take advantage of the privacy settings available in your Metaverse software to control who can see your profile and other information, and adjust them as necessary.

7 Report suspicious activity: If you encounter any suspicious activity or content in the Metaverse, report it to the relevant authorities, such as the Metaverse platform provider or law enforcement, as soon as possible.

By following these steps, you can reduce your risk and increase your safety in the Metaverse.

Attention!!

Sports Trading is Here!

Sports trading, also known as sports investing or sports betting, has witnessed significant growth and popularity in recent years. This practice involves the buying and selling of sports-related assets, such as bets, contracts, and shares, with the aim of generating profits. With the advent of online platforms and advanced data analytics, sports trading has transformed into a sophisticated and lucrative industry. Let us explore the evolution, impact, and future of **Sports Trading**.

Evolution of Sports Trading

Sports trading has come a long way from its early origins as a recreational pastime to a professional and data-driven activity. The rise of online platforms has provided accessibility and convenience to sports traders worldwide. Gone are the days when bettors relied solely on intuition and luck. Today, sports traders employ statistical models, algorithmic analysis, and machine learning techniques to make informed investment decisions.

The advent of in-play or live betting has revolutionized sports trading. With realtime data and instant updates, traders can react to changing game dynamics, capitalize on market inefficiencies, and exploit valuable trading opportunities. The integration of sports trading with technology has allowed for greater liquidity, transparency, and speed in executing trades, attracting both amateur and professional traders alike.

Impact of Sports Trading

Sports trading has emerged as a multi-billion-dollar industry, generating significant economic activity. It has created job opportunities, fostered entrepreneurship, and contributed to tax revenues in many jurisdictions. Sports trading also drives ancillary industries such as data analytics, software development, and media coverage.

Sports Integrity

The rise of sports trading has brought attention to the issue of sports integrity. With large sums of money at stake, the potential for match-fixing and corruption increases. However, sports trading platforms have implemented stringent regulations, monitoring mechanisms, and collaboration with sports organizations to combat these risks. This emphasis on integrity has led to increased scrutiny and awareness, thereby enhancing the overall credibility of sports.

Fan Engagement

Sports trading has transformed the way fans engage with sports. It adds an extra layer of excitement and involvement, as individuals can now have a financial stake in the outcome of a game. This increased engagement has spurred interest and viewership, leading to enhanced fan experiences and higher revenues for sports organizations.

Data Analytics and Innovation

The development of sports trading has prompted advancements in data analytics and technology. Traders harness vast amounts of data, including player performance, team statistics, and historical trends to gain a competitive edge. This demand for data has propelled the growth of sports analytics, leading to innovations in tracking technologies, wearable devices, and performance metrics.

Future Prospects

The future of sports trading holds immense potential for further growth and innovation. Here are some key areas to watch:

Expansion of Market Offerings

Sports trading is no longer limited to traditional sports like football, basketball, or tennis. The emergence of niche markets such as esports, fantasy sports, and virtual competitions presents new trading opportunities and markets for investors.

Artificial Intelligence and Machine Learning

Advancements in artificial intelligence and machine learning will continue to play a crucial role in sports trading. Predictive models and algorithms will become more sophisticated, enabling traders to make more accurate and profitable decisions. One of the best I have found is Lance Green, based in Brazil. They have incredible rewards and incentives. To learn more about Lance Green, go to: https://linktr. ee/Lance.green Watch the 8-minute, LGreen, Overview video. PW 8888. Then follow this link to your dreams: https://app.lgreen.ai/join/ psalm1vf

Regulatory Frameworks

As the sports trading industry evolves, regulators will likely develop comprehensive frameworks to ensure consumer protection, fair play, and responsible gambling practices. Collaboration between sports organizations, governments, and trading platforms will be the key to strike a balance between innovation and regulation.

IN CONCLUSION

Financial satisfaction is not a one-time achievement, but rather a continuous process of learning. Whether you are considering investing in precious metals or cryptocurrencies, the key to reducing fear and anxiety is education. By learning more about these investment options, you will gain a deeper understanding of the risks and potential rewards involved. This will give you the confidence you need to make informed investment decisions and pursue your financial goals with greater ease. Remember, education trumps fear every time, and the more you know about your investments, the better equipped you will be to make decisions that will lead to success. Living on a modern-day financial plantation is a reality for many individuals and communities in the United States and around the world. It operates through predatory lending practices and systemic discrimination, trapping individuals and communities in a cycle of debt and poverty. Addressing these issues requires systemic changes, including stronger consumer protections and greater access to wealth-building opportunities for marginalized communities. Only then can we begin to break the cycle of poverty and financial instability and build a more equitable and just society. The modern-day financial plantation can be a difficult cycle to break, but it is possible. By educating themselves, creating a budget, saving, and investing, individuals can take control of their finances and build a better future. The key is to start small and make incremental changes, building momentum over time. With hard work, dedication, and the right tools, anyone can escape the modern-day financial plantation and secure their financial future. Deciding which way to invest should be based on your individual goals and circumstances. Some investors use Precious Metals IRAs for their retirement savings while also keeping additional metals stored at home or in a safe.

Cryptocurrency is a decentralized digital currency that uses cryptography to secure its transactions and control the creation of new units. The first and most well-known cryptocurrency is Bitcoin, which was created in 2009. Since then, hundreds of other cryptocurrencies have been created, each with its own unique features and uses.

The rise of cryptocurrency has been meteoric, and many people are now looking for ways to ride the wave and make a profit. However, investing in cryptocurrency can be risky, and it is important to approach it with caution and a well-informed strategy.

NFTs are a fascinating development in the world of digital assets and creativity. They are a tool for creators to monetize their work, a platform for collectors to invest in unique digital assets, and a symbol of the shifting landscape of digital ownership. To me, they represent a new and exciting way to engage with digital art and creativity, and they have the potential to greatly impact the future of digital assets and ownership. To learn more about NFTs. Go to: https://qualitynft.me

The metaverse represents an exciting vision of a connected virtual world, offering immersive experiences and limitless possibilities. While it is still a concept under development, its potential impact on various aspects of our lives cannot be underestimated. As we navigate the path toward the metaverse, it is essential to consider the ethical, societal, and technological implications to ensure its responsible and inclusive growth. When combined with other platforms like Gaming, and Networking. The Metaverse has unlimited possibilities. To learn more, go to: https://earn.starhorizon.net/en/quality1/ph/star/ref-customer/LEFT

Or Email: psalm1vf@gmail.com

Sports trading has evolved from a recreational hobby to a sophisticated industry with a significant economic impact, enhanced sports integrity, and increased fan engagement. The integration of technology, data analytics, and innovation has propelled the growth of this sector, with promising prospects for the future. As sports trading continues to evolve, it is vital to strike a balance between innovation, integrity, and responsible trading practices to ensure its long-term sustainability and positive impact on the world of sports. To learn more about Lance Green, go to: https://linktr.ee/Lance.greenWatch the 8-minute, LGreen, Overview video. PW 8888. Then follow this link to your dreams:https://app.lgreen.ai/join/psalm1vf

"Multiple Streams of Income, Education, and Good Health are the Keys to Becoming "Financially

Free/Truly Wealthy"! Faith and Trust in Your Heavenly Father Will Lead to a Life of Abundance and Wellness!"

Brother Willie"

ABOUT THE AUTHOR

Willie L. Davis Sr. is a financially independent, online marketing entrepreneur sharing knowledge with the world about true financial freedom. Willie is constantly establishing win/win connections and global relationships daily. He will never miss an opportunity to checkout your spiritual health by asking the question, "Are you ready, today, for ETERNITY?" Willie has two master degrees, retired early at 49, and lives in the Philippine Islands with his wife Aura, and three kids, Teaura, Chantell, and Willie Davis Jr. He's the Director of a 501 (c) 3, nonprofit, kid's charity, Psalm 1 Victory Foundation, Inc., a global outreach feeding ministry registered in the U.S. and operating in the Philippines, under the same name.

Willie is also a Vietnam era veteran, who served during the first Gulf War, up to and including the Iraq War. He retired as an E-9, from the Pentagon, after 25 years of service in the U. S. Air Force. In addition, he retired from the Department of Defense, Civil Service, as a GS-13, after serving as the Director of Transportation, Air National Guard Bureau.

Willie is a world traveler who says that his year living in Thailand was only topped by the three years he lived in the Mediterranean on the Island of Crete, Greece. These world experiences brings a freshness to his writing and add a global financial perspective. Willie writes from the heart and has an overwhelming desire to see others succeed. Willie brings 20 years of financial analysis, and debt counseling experience to the table. Amazingly, he foresaw the market crash of 2008 coming, and got out at the TOP of the Real Estate market in 2006! This visionary author is now sharing his insights and secrets with the world!

Other achievements: Successful Real Estate Investor; Licensed Air Frame & Power

Plant Mechanic; Series 6, 63 Securities Representative, & 26 Licensed Principal;

Master Crew Chief, multiple aircraft series, to include the B-52, KC-135, and C141; Certified Logistician; Production Controller; Powered Support Equipment Manager; Telecommunication's Computer and Radio Operator; Certified (TQM) Total Quality Management Instructor; Selected as a Civilian to attend the military's Air Command and Staff College (ACSC); Awarded the Meritorious Service Medal; Received a personal invitation to the White House in 2001. Three times retired with multiple streams of income. To learn more about Willie L. Davis Sr., please visit **www.willieldavis.com.**

BIBLIOGRAPHY

Alternative Medicine – Sunday, July 26, 2009

American Medical Association

Hill, Napoleon, Think and Grow Rich

King James Version of the Bible

Prater, Connie, CreditCards.com, Issuer of 79.9% interest rate credit card defends its product

Stewart, Emily, Poughkeepsie Journal 5:08 p.m. EDT June 5, 2014

Wikipedia, the free encyclopedia

Williams, Art, Common Sense, Primerica Financial Services, Inc. @ 1983, @1994

www.ingramcontent.com/pod-product-compliance
Lightning Source LLC
Chambersburg PA
CBHW071658210326
41597CB00017B/2240